Foreplay

A Book of Appeteasers

by

Chef Eliza

Aug 10/09!

For the queen of appetizers! Here's to many more gourmet treats together!

amor, Mark & Romi xo

Copyright © Eliza Gavin, 2006

All rights reserved. No part of this book may be reproduced or transmitted in any form or by any means, electronic or mechanical, including photocopying, recording, or by any information storage and retrieval system, without permission in writing from the publisher.

ISBN: 0-9776513-0-4

For more information write to:

Goodall L.L.C.
PO Box 1158,
Telluride, Colorado 81435

This book is dedicated to John Patton,

Who taught me that the secret ingredient to every recipe is love

And to my husband Gavin who taught me what love is.

To Karen,
Happy 50th
Birthday!

To Karen,
Happy 50th
Birthday!

Contents

Introduction 9

Vegetarian Canapés

Miniature Cabbage and Roasted Shallot Quiches 12
Marinated Goat Cheese with Lentil Salad on Anadama Toasts 14
White Bean, Red Onion and Basil Stuffed Cherry Tomatoes 16
Roasted Jalapeños with Corn and Cheddar Stuffing .17
Split Green Pea Patties with Tomato Yogurt Dipping Sauce 18
Marinated Asparagus with Smoked Gouda and Eggplant 20
Black Bean Cakes with Beet Cream 22
Caramelized Apricot Slices with Camembert on Pumpernickel Toasts 23
Leek and Carrot Rolls Stuffed with Fennel and Comté
      Dressed with Champagne Vinaigrette 25
Spinach Rolls with Basil, Mozzarella and Tomato Confit 26
Cantaloupe and Papaya Slices with Goat Cheese on Carrot Nut Bread 28
Glazed Radishes with Black Bean Purée 29
Red Cabbage Chiffonade with Apple Chutney and Walnuts on Herb Toasts 31

Fish

Anchovy Wrapped Capers with Mozzarella
      and Olive Tapenade on Zucchini Slices 34
Smoked Trout and Tomato Quiches 35
Trout with Avocado Purée on Sesame Crackers 37
Catfish Nuggets with Raspberry Dipping Sauce 39
Catfish and Basil Sausage with Cantaloupe Sauce on Sesame Pita Chips 40
Cured Salmon with Fennel Cream on Cucumber Slices 42
Smoked Salmon Cakes with Jalapeño Tartar 43
Spinach, Carrot and Beet Terrine of Sole with Cumin Sesame Crackers 44
Poached Halibut with Tarragon Sauce and Lettuce Leaves on Walnut Toasts 47
Potato Crusted Halibut with Fennel Relish on Sour Cream Toasts 49
Prosciutto Stuffed Halibut with Radicchio on Cornmeal Toasts 51
Spicy Tuna with Carrot and Cucumber Slaw on Chapati Crisps 53
Tuna Nori Rolls with Carrot, Radish, Avocado and Tobiko 55
Green Peppercorn Crusted Tuna with Wasabi Aioli on Carrot Crackers 56

Mahi Mahi with Mango Salsa and Caper Aioli on Crusty Buttermilk Toasts 58
Pita Wraps of Sesame Mahi Mahi with Watercress 60
Fish Cakes with Tropical Dipping Sauce 62
Poppy Seed Dusted Sea Bass with Radish Slaw on Wonton Chips 64

Shellfish

Oysters Baked on the Half Shell with Tarragon and Bacon Cream Sauce 66
Oysters Served on the Half Shell with Roasted Beet Vinaigrette 67
Oyster, Bacon and Carrot Brochettes with Caper Tartar 68
Pickled Clams with Tomato and Oregano Relish on Wonton Chips 70
Fresh Herb Clam Stuffing on Bagel Chips with Roasted Red Peppers 72
Clam and Corn Fritters with Blue Cheese and Basil Dressing 74
Glazed Shrimp with Oregano Roasted Shallots on French Bread 75
Rock Shrimp Wontons with Spicy Honey 77
Boiled Crawfish with Cantaloupe Papaya Salad on Sesame Crackers 78
Green Crawfish Cakes with Roasted Red Pepper Aioli .80
Crab Tempura with Spicy Tomato Dipping Sauce 81
Crabmeat, Capers and Fennel Stuffed in Mushroom Caps 83
Crab Salad in Lettuce Pouches 84
Basil and Pink Grapefruit Scallops with Mixed Greens on Anise Crackers 85
Cardamom Scallops with Celeriac Purée on Brown Bread 86
Spicy Glazed Scallops 88
Scallop Seviche with Tomato and Avocado Salsa on Whole Wheat Toasts 89
Miso Lobster with Endive Chiffonade in Choux Pastry 91
Steamed Mussels with Cucumber Cardamom Sauce 93

Poultry

Julienne of Chicken Breast with Braised Caper
    and Tomato Sauce on Fresh Herb Focaccia 96
Chicken Egg Rolls with Apricot Sauce 98
Chicken Breast and Carrot Rolls 100
Ginger Chicken with Radicchio and Lentil Salad on Sweet Toasts 102
Chicken and Grapefruit Salad in Oat Rolls 104

Tarragon Chicken Wings with Caper Mayonnaise 106
Smoked Chicken Salad in Endive Leaves 108
Spicy Turkey Breast with Cantaloupe on Parmesan Toasts 109
Turkey Patties with Tomato Confit and Scallion Aioli on Basil Bagels 111
Smoked Turkey Breast with Sweet Beet Slices
    on Half-Cracked Black Pepper Crackers 114
Turkey Kibbe Kebabs with Mint Basil Dressing 116

Beef and Lamb

Skirt Steak with Mango Salsa 118
Beef, Pecan and Radicchio Strudel 119
Beef Tenderloin, Corn Salsa and Jack Cheese Quesadillas 120
Beef Tenderloin with Fresh Herb Pesto on Oregano Biscuits 122
Beef Tenderloin with Tomato and Caper Relish on Chili Bagels 124
Braised Beef and Carrots with Bibb Lettuce in French Rolls 126
Sesame and Black Pepper Crusted Beef
    with Carrot and Endive Slaw on Pita Chips 128
Mint Pesto Stuffed Lamb with Shaved Fennel 130
Sliced Loin of Lamb with Oregano Hummus on Pumpkin Crackers 132

Pork

Barbecue Pork with Pineapple Sage Salsa on Goat Cheese Biscuits 136
Celeriac Purée with Shiitake Mushrooms and Rendered Bacon in Phyllo Dough 138
Prosciutto and Goat Cheese Wrapped Cantaloupe Slices 139
Coconut Pork with Basil and Mango on Pita Chips 140
Pork Tenderloin Stuffed with Sage, Salami, Asparagus and Roasted Red Peppers 142
Asparagus, Basil, Mozzarella and Serrano Ham Rolls 143
Cantaloupe and Papaya Salad with Prosciutto in Plums 144
Fresh Herb Pâté with Oregano Mustard on Gouda-Thyme Bread 145
Oregano Sausage with Tomatoes and Olive Tapenade on Cheese Biscuits 147

Game

Quail Tamales with Tomato and Avocado Salsa 150
Fried Quail Legs with Spicy Lemon Grass Sauce 152
Roasted Quail with Avocado and Tomato Cream on Tomatillo Tortilla Chips ..154
Smoked Pheasant with Hummus on Parmesan Biscuits 156

Sliced Rabbit with Carrot Relish on Rye Toasts 158
Rabbit, Tarragon and Sunflower Seed Terrine
     with Glazed Parsnips on Dill Toasts 160
Rabbit Sausage with Garlic Roasted Shallots on Oregano Focaccia 162
Buffalo Patties with Radicchio Sauce on Cilantro Pita Chips 165
Cajun Smoked Duck Breast with Fennel on Tangy Chive Toasts 167
Duck Sausage Rolls with Sweet Mustard Sauce 169
Confit of Duck with Spinach and Basil in Phyllo Dough 171

After-anecdote 173

Appetite-Stimulating Ingredients 174

Introduction

When I was a young girl in Richmond, Virginia, my father would take the family to a delightful French restaurant called *La Petit France*. A native of France, Chef Paul still produces some of the most delicious morsels ever to touch my palate.

Paul's wife, Marie, is an enchanting woman with Parisian clothes that drive the women of Richmond mad with jealousy. Marie would care for the guests with amusing anecdotes and kisses on each cheek.

One of our visits occurred on the eve of Thanksgiving. When Marie came to our table, we inquired about her and Paul's plans for Thanksgiving dinner. She told us that Paul was preparing a feast in the American tradition with a French twist.

"Are you having turkey with gravy?" my father asked. "No," Marie replied in her heavy accent, "In France we do not have gravy, we have sauce!"

This is one of the many experiences that formed my belief system in the culinary arts. I believe the purpose of the canapé is to wet one's palate, not to drown it. The canapé is the first act in a murder mystery. By stuffing the diner before the main course, the host tells the viewer the murderer and the motive. Therefore I have constructed these recipes that contain appetite stimulating ingredients. With these canapés your guests will anticipate the next course instead of feeling overwhelmed.

I find the power of food to be truly amazing. Food is so much more than filling an empty stomach. It makes us alert, pensive, aggressive or gives us energy. Ingredients act as diuretics, stimulants and tonics. Food has the ability to lift our mood or put us to sleep. Ingredients relieve depression or behave as antispasmodics. Certain foods reduce some allergy symptoms.

Ingredients also have a lasting effect on the eater. Science dictates that an extended period of consumption of red meat causes arteries to clog. My pregnant mother was served a dinner of scrambled eggs and lemon gelatin by my well meaning father. She went into labor that evening and produced a beautiful baby boy. To this day, my brother detests eggs or gelatin in any form.

Food's power should not be disregarded but rather manipulated to our benefit. A good host needs to investigate the benefits and the setbacks of ingredients and use them in proper situations. For this reason we do not serve our guests beef stew at our pool parties.

After extensive research of the effect of nutrients on the body, I found several ingredients known to stimulate the appetite. Some foods improve the sense of smell, which helps to stimulate the appetite. The vitamins and minerals in some ingredients stimulate the appetites of persons who have had difficulty feeling hungry. Some vegetables cleanse the system so effectively, they stimulate the appetite.

I designed this book to aid the host. Please mix and match the different proteins, condiments, breads or crackers. Feel free to buy crackers, loaves of bread or canned beans. All of the bread and cracker recipes can be made with a standing mixer and a dough hook. This book does not tell you what to do, rather what you can do. I enjoyed writing the recipes and the anecdotes for *Foreplay: A Book of Appeteasers* and I hope you and your guests find it entertaining.

Vegetarian Canapés

After I finished university, I spent the summer in a small college town. I rented an apartment that sat on the west bluff of a mountain. My landlord, Gordie, was a simple countryman with an aversion for waste. Gordie constructed my duplex and another house from recycled materials. The house had a beautiful marble mantel from a torn down chapel and my hardwood floors were once a basketball court.

The summer before I rented, Gordie had cultivated one-half acre of my front yard into a giant vegetable garden. He lovingly grew his vegetables, but had only a small family to feed. Determined to help Gordie with his surplus, I declared myself a vegetarian for the summer. Gordie left the remainder of his huge crop in buckets on my front porch. Everyday was a new 10 gallon bucket of freshly picked delights.

The summer began with cucumbers. I then received a mountain of squash and zucchini, followed by a flood of sweet corn. Gordie would arrive at my porch door with his arms full of basil bouquets. My windowsills and railings teemed with ripening tomatoes. At the end of summer I threw a watermelon party in which each guest received their own personal watermelon.

It was a beautiful summer and if given the opportunity to consume vegetables still dirty from the soil, I would dedicate myself to a life of vegetarianism.

Miniature Cabbage and Roasted Shallot Quiches

Makes 36 Quiches

Quiche Crusts

1/2 cup cold, unsalted butter (and more for muffin tins)
1 teaspoon salt
1 1/4 cups all purpose flour
1 egg
2 teaspoons water

1. Finely chop the butter into the flour and salt. Rub the butter, salt and flour between one's hands or pulse the ingredients in a food processor until they resemble a coarse meal. Form this mixture into a well. Add the egg and water to the center of the well. Gradually combine the wet and dry ingredients. Add a few more drops of water until the dough comes together. Do not over work the dough or it will be tough. Cover the dough with plastic wrap and place it in the refrigerator for 30 minutes.

2. Generously butter and flour 3 muffin pans. If you do not have 3 muffin pans, work in batches. Place the pans in the refrigerator while rolling out the dough. On a floured surface, roll the dough 1/4-inch thick. With a round cookie cutter, cut circles out of the dough. Place one dough circle in each of the muffin hollows. Insure there is no air between the crust and the pan. With a fork, prick holes in the dough. Chill the crusts in the freezer for 30 minutes.

3. Preheat the oven to 350°F. Line each crust with parchment paper. Fill the paper with dried beans. Place the crusts in the oven for 5-8 minutes. Remove the beans and parchment paper. This technique is called blind baking. It ensures nice, crispy crusts and fillings that are moist and not over cooked. The beans prevent the dough from rising during the baking process.

Roasted Shallots

5 shallots, unpeeled
1 tablespoon olive oil

1. Preheat the oven to 400°F. Place the shallots in a roasting pan. Toss the shallots in the olive oil and place them in the oven. Allow the shallots to roast for 20 minutes. Cool the shallots.

2. Remove the skins and roots from the shallots and slice them thinly.

Cabbage

1 small Savoy cabbage
1 tablespoon unsalted butter
1 teaspoon salt
1/2 teaspoon white pepper
1/4 cup fresh sage leaves, chopped

1. Halve the cabbage and remove the core. Finely chop the cabbage. Remove any dirt by swishing the cabbage in a bowl of cold water. Plunge the cabbage in a pot of boiling, salted water for 2 minutes. Strain the cabbage and place it in a shallow pan with the butter, salt and pepper. Place the pan over a medium heat. Cook the cabbage for 15 minutes or until it is tender. Remove the cabbage from the heat and add the sage. Allow the cabbage to cool completely.

Quiche Custard

2 cups heavy cream
3 eggs
1 teaspoon salt
1/2 teaspoon dark chili powder
3/4 cup Parmesan cheese, grated

Preheat the oven to 350°F. Whisk the cream, eggs, salt and chili powder. Place a spoonful of cabbage and 1 teaspoon of Parmesan cheese in a quiche crust. Pour the custard to 3/4 the height of the crust and top it with a few roasted shallot slices. Repeat this process with the rest of the quiches. Bake the quiches for 10-15 minutes. When an inserted toothpick comes out clean they are done. Serve the quiches warm or chilled.

Marinated Goat Cheese with Lentil Salad on Anadama Toasts

Marinated Goat Cheese

8 ounces goat cheese
2 garlic cloves, finely chopped
1 bay leaf
3 peppercorns
1 shallot, finely chopped
3 thyme sprigs
2 dried chili peppers
2 cups extra virgin olive oil

Form the goat cheese into 40 quarter sized patties. Place the patties and the remaining ingredients in a sealed container. Allow the goat cheese to marinate for 12-36 hours. Remove the patties from the marinade. Strain the marinade and use the oil for salad dressings and marinades.

Anadama Toasts

1 teaspoon dry active yeast
2 tablespoons warm water, 105-115°F
1 tablespoon shortening
1 tablespoon salt
2 1/4 cups all purpose flour
1/2 teaspoon granulated sugar
3/4 cup water
2 tablespoons blackstrap molasses
1/4 cup cornmeal

1. Sprinkle the yeast and sugar over the warm water. Let this mixture stand in a warm place until it is foamy, about 10 minutes.

2. In a pot over a medium heat combine the remaining water, shortening, molasses and salt. Heat to 105-115°F. Add this mixture to the yeast mixture.

3. Whisk the cornmeal into the yeast mixture. Stir the flour into the yeast mixture, one cup at a time. Turn this sticky dough out onto a floured surface. Knead the dough until it is smooth, elastic and still a little sticky, about 10 minutes. Place the dough in an oiled bowl and flip it to oil all sides. Cover the dough and allow it to rise in a warm place until it has doubled in bulk.

4. Preheat the oven to 425°F. Gently deflate the dough. Shape the dough into 2 narrow loaves. Place the loaves on a parchment paper lined baking sheet. Cover the loaves and allow them to rise until they have doubled in bulk.

5. Bake the loaves for 10 minutes. Reduce the heat to 350°F and bake the loaves for an additional 35 minutes. Cool the loaves completely on a grill.

5. Preheat the broiler. Slice the loaves thinly and toast them under the broiler until they are crisp.

Lentil Salad

1 stalk fresh lemon grass
2 cups lentils
3 cups water
1/2 cup yellow onion, finely chopped
1 dried red chili
2 garlic cloves, chopped
1 tablespoon fresh ginger, peeled and chopped
2 tomatoes
2 heads of endive
Juice of 1 lemon

1. Place the lemon grass on a cutting board. With the smooth side of a mallet or small pot, smash the white end of the stalk until it comes apart. Chop the white end and discard the green. Place the lentils, water, onion, chili, garlic, ginger and lemon grass in a pot over a high heat. When the liquid boils, reduce the heat to medium-low. Gently simmer the lentils for 1 hour or until they are soft, adding water as needed. Remove the chili and allow the lentils to cool.

2. Core the tomatoes. With a paring knife, mark the bottom of each tomato with an X. Plunge the tomatoes in a pot of boiling water for 1 minute or until their skins begin to come off. Transfer the tomatoes to a bowl of ice water. When they are completely cool, peel the skins from the tomatoes. Remove the seeds and membranes and finely chop the tomatoes. Add the tomatoes to the lentils

3. Wash the endive leaves (do not allow them to soak in water, as this tends to enhance their bitterness). Crosscut the endive leaves and add them to the lentils. Add the lemon juice to the lentil salad. Add salt and pepper to taste.

4. Place a spoonful of lentil salad on an Anadama toast. Top the lentils with a goat cheese wedge. Repeat this process with the remaining goat cheese patties.

White Bean, Red Onion and Basil Stuffed Cherry Tomatoes

Makes 30 Tomatoes

1 cup dried white beans
2 thyme sprigs
1 dried chili
1 teaspoon dill seed
1 small red onion, finely chopped
1 teaspoon black pepper
2 tablespoons balsamic vinegar
1/4 cup extra virgin olive oil
Additional basil for garnish

1/2 yellow onion, finely chopped
1 bay leaf
2 garlic cloves, chopped
3 cups water
1/4 cup fresh basil leaves, finely chopped
1 teaspoon salt
1 tablespoon lemon juice
30 cherry tomatoes

1. Rinse the beans and pick out any stones. Soak the beans in cold water for 12 hours. Drain the beans and place them in a pot with the yellow onion, thyme, bay leaf, chili, garlic, dill seed and water. Place the pot over a medium-high heat. Bring the beans to a boil and reduce the heat to medium. Adding water as needed, simmer the beans for 2 hours or until they are soft. Discard the thyme, bay leaf and chili. Strain the beans and cool them completely.

2. Whisk together the red onion, chopped basil, pepper, salt, vinegar, lemon juice and olive oil. Pour this dressing over the beans and allow the beans to marinate for 1-4 hours.

3. Cut off the tops of each cherry tomato. With a melon baller, hollow out the inside of each tomato. Stuff the tomatoes with the bean salad and top them with chopped basil. Serve the tomatoes chilled.

Roasted Jalapeños with Corn and Cheddar Stuffing

Makes 20 Canapés

2 ears sweet corn
2 garlic cloves, minced
1/4 cup fresh cilantro leaves, finely chopped
1/2 cup shredded cheddar cheese
1 teaspoon salt
2 tablespoons olive oil

2 tomatoes
1/2 cup fresh parsley leaves, finely chopped
4 scallions, green parts only, finely chopped
1/4 cup cottage cheese
20 jalapeños

1. Remove the husks and any silks from the ears of corn. Place the ears in a pot of boiling water and cover them. Allow the ears to cook for 3-5 minutes. At the end of cooking, add a pinch of salt. Salt tends to toughen the kernels if added at the beginning of cooking. Strain the ears. When the corn is cool, cut the kernels off of the cobs.

2. Core each tomato and mark the bottoms with X's. Plunge the tomatoes in a pot of boiling water. Leave them for 1 minute or until the skins begin to come off. Transfer the tomatoes to a bath of ice water. When the tomatoes are completely cool, remove their skins, seeds and membranes. Finely chop the tomatoes.

3. Combine the corn, tomatoes, garlic, parsley, cilantro, scallions, cheddar cheese, cottage cheese and salt.

4. Wash the jalapeños. I recommend wearing rubber gloves when working with chilies. Cut the stems off of the jalapeños. With a paring knife scrape out any seeds and membranes. Using a pastry bag or spoon, stuff each of the peppers with the corn mixture.

5. Preheat the oven to 350°F. Place a pan over a medium-high heat. Working in batches, heat 1 tablespoon of the olive oil. When the oil is hot, place a few of the peppers in the pan. Turn the peppers as their skins blister. Repeat this process with the remaining peppers, adding oil when necessary. When their skins are completely blistered, place the Jalapeños in the oven. Allow the peppers to roast for 10 minutes or until the cheese melts. Serve the Jalapeños warm.

Split Green Pea Patties with Tomato Yogurt Dipping Sauce

Tomato Yogurt Dipping Sauce

2 tomatoes
1 shallot, minced
1 tablespoon rice wine vinegar
1 cup plain yogurt

1. Core the tomatoes. With a paring knife, mark the bottom of each tomato with an X. Plunge the tomatoes in a pot of boiling water for 1 minute or until their skins begin to come off. Transfer the tomatoes to a bowl of ice water. When they are completely cool, remove their skins and seeds and finely chop the tomato flesh.

2. In a blender or food processor, purée the shallot, tomato and vinegar. Add the yogurt and continue to blend. Allow the flavors to marry for 1 hour. Strain the sauce.

Split Green Peas

2 cups dried split green peas
1/4 cup chopped yellow onion
2 garlic cloves, minced
1/2 teaspoon ground cardamom
1 tablespoon ground cumin seed
1 teaspoon cayenne pepper
1 tablespoon dark chili powder
2 cups water

1. Soak the split peas in cold water, for 4 hours. Drain the peas and pick out any stones.

2. Place the peas and the remaining ingredients in a pot, over a high heat. When the mixture boils, reduce the heat to medium-low. Partially cover the pot and let the ingredients simmer for 30 minutes or until the peas are tender. Add more water as needed. Strain the peas of any liquid and cool.

Split Green Pea Patties

3/4 cup yellow onion, chopped
1 tablespoon sesame oil
2 Poblano chilies, cored and seeded and finely chopped
1 teaspoon white pepper
1/4 cup fresh cilantro leaves
1/4 cup flat leaf parsley leaves
2 tablespoons lemon juice
1 1/2 cups breadcrumbs
3 tablespoons corn oil

1. Over a medium-high heat sauté the onions in the sesame oil, for 10 minutes or until they are brown. In a food processor, purée the cooked pea mixture with the onions. Scrape down the sides of the bowl and add the chilies, pepper, cilantro and parsley. Purée the ingredients until they are smooth. Transfer the batter to a mixing bowl. Add the lemon juice and breadcrumbs. Form 2 tablespoons of the batter into a small patty. Repeat this process with the remaining batter. Refrigerate the patties for 30 minutes.

2. Heat 1 tablespoon of the corn oil over a medium-high heat in a deep pan. When the oil is hot add a few of the patties. Cook the patties for 3 minutes on each side or until they are brown. Place the patties on paper towels to remove any excess grease. Repeat this process with the remaining patties. Serve the patties warm or chilled with the sauce on the side.

Marinated Asparagus with Smoked Gouda and Eggplant

Marinated Asparagus

1 bunch of thin asparagus spears
1 shallot, finely chopped
2 green onions, green parts only, finely chopped
2 tablespoons flat leaf parsley leaves, finely chopped
2 garlic cloves, finely chopped
2 tablespoons balsamic vinegar
A pinch of salt
1 teaspoon black pepper
1/4 cup olive oil
1 head of fennel, cored and finely chopped
1 large tomato, very ripe
1/4 cup capers
1/4 cup fresh basil leaves, chopped

1. Remove the woody ends of the asparagus spears by grasping a spear by both ends and bending it until it snaps. Discard the root end of the spear. Repeat this process with the remaining asparagus. Cut the spears into halves. Plunge the asparagus spears into boiling, salted water for 5 minutes or until they are tender. Transfer the spears to a bowl of ice water. When the asparagus spears have cooled completely, strain them and pat them dry.

2. In a bowl, whisk together the shallot, green onions, parsley, garlic, balsamic vinegar, salt, pepper and 1 cup of the olive oil. Pour the marinade over the asparagus spears. Marinate the spears for 4 hours.

3. Place the fennel in a shallow pan with 1 tablespoon of the olive oil. Place the pan over a medium-high heat and sweat the fennel until it is tender, about 10 minutes.

4. Core the tomato. With a paring knife, mark the bottom of the tomato with an X. Plunge the tomato in a pot of boiling water for 1 minute or until the skin begins to come off. Transfer the tomato to a bowl of ice water. When it is completely cool, peel the skin from the tomato. Remove its seeds and finely chop the tomato.

5. In a bowl, combine the fennel, tomato, capers and basil. Remove the asparagus from the marinade. After straining the marinade, it can be used as a salad dressing.

Eggplant

2 eggplants, peeled
Kosher salt
3 tablespoons olive oil
8 ounces smoked Gouda

1. Crosscut the eggplants into 1/4-inch thick rounds. Place the slices in a colander. Cover the slices with kosher salt and drain them for 20 minutes. Rinse the salt off of the slices and pat them dry on paper towels.

2. Place a pan over a medium-high heat. When the pan is hot add 1 tablespoon of the olive oil. Working in batches, sauté the slices for about 3 minutes on each side, or until they are cooked through but not falling apart. Repeat this process with the remaining slices, adding oil as needed. Cool the eggplant.

2. Cut the smoked Gouda into thick matchsticks. Beginning on an edge of an eggplant round, place a matchstick of smoked Gouda. Place a few asparagus spears on the cheese and top with 1 tablespoon of the fennel mixture. Wrap the eggplant around the asparagus and vegetables and into a roll. Secure the roll with a toothpick. Serve the canapés chilled. You can also pop these in a hot oven to melt the cheese and serve them warm.

Black Bean Cakes with Beet Cream

Black Bean Cakes

2 cups black beans
1 tablespoon dark chili powder
2 garlic cloves, chopped
1 teaspoon freshly ground black pepper
1/2 cup banana peppers, chopped
1 cup breadcrumbs
1 tablespoon sesame oil

2 thyme sprigs
1 teaspoon ground cumin
1 bay leaf
2 carrots, peeled and chopped
1/2 cup fresh basil leaves
1/4 cup olive oil

1. Soak the black beans in cold water for 8 hours. Drain the beans and place them in a pot. Fill the pot with enough water to cover the beans by two inches. Add the thyme, chili powder, cumin, garlic, bay leaf and black pepper to the beans. Place the beans over a high heat. When the beans boil, reduce the heat to medium-low. Adding water as needed, simmer the beans for 3 hours or until they are tender. Drain the beans and cool them.

2. In a food processor, purée the beans, carrots, banana peppers, and basil. Add salt to taste. Stir in the breadcrumbs 1/4 cup at a time, until the mixture is firm.

3. Heat the olive and sesame oils together in a shallow pan over a medium-high heat. Spoon 2 tablespoons of bean mixture into the hot oil. Flatten the bean cake with a spatula. Sauté the bean cake for 3 minutes on each side. Working in batches, repeat this process with the remaining batter. Pat the cakes with paper towels to remove any excess grease.

Beet Cream

3 beets
1/2 cup whipping cream
1 tablespoon granulated sugar

3 tablespoons raspberry vinegar
1 tablespoon sour cream

1. Preheat the oven to 400°F. Remove the greens from the beets. Gently scrub the beets under cold water until they are free of dirt. Dry the beets and place them in a roasting pan. Place the beets in the oven and roast them for 30 minutes. When the skins of the beets are ballooning, the beets have finished roasting. Let the beets stand until they are cool enough to handle.

2. Under cold, running water remove the skins from the beets. Coarsely chop the beets.

3. Place beets, raspberry vinegar, whipping cream, sour cream and sugar in a blender. Blend the ingredients until they are smooth.

4. Serve the black bean cakes warm with the beet cream on the side.

Caramelized Apricot Slices with Camembert on Pumpernickel Toasts

Makes 30 Canapés

Pumpernickel Toasts

1 teaspoon dry active yeast
1/4 teaspoon granulated sugar
1/4 cup warm water, 105-115°F
1/2 cup cold water
1 cup cornmeal
3/4 cup boiling water
1 teaspoon salt
1 teaspoon unsalted butter
1 teaspoon caraway seeds
1/2 cup mashed potatoes
1 cup rye flour
1 cup all purpose flour

1. Sprinkle the yeast and sugar over the warm water. Allow the yeast to rise in a warm, draft free area for 10 minutes, or until it is foamy.

2. In a pot, whisk the cold water into the cornmeal. Add the boiling water and place the cornmeal over a medium heat. Constantly stirring, cook the cornmeal until it is thick, 7-10 minutes. Pour the cornmeal into a large mixing bowl. Whisk the salt, butter and caraway seeds into the cornmeal and allow this mixture to cool. Incorporate the mashed potatoes and yeast mixture with the cornmeal. Stir in the flours one cup at a time. When the flours are incorporated, turn the dough out onto a floured surface. Knead the dough for 10 minutes or until it is smooth and elastic. Place the dough in an oiled bowl and flip it to oil all sides. Allow the dough to rise in a warm draft free area, until it has doubled in bulk.

4. Preheat the oven to 425°F. Gently punch down the dough and shape it into two loaves. Place the loaves on a well greased baking sheet. Cover the loaves and allow them to rise in a draft free area, until they have doubled in bulk.

5. Place the loaves in the oven for 10 minutes. Reduce the heat to 350°F and allow the loaves to bake an additional 40 minutes. Place the loaves on a grill to cool.

6. Cut the loaves into 1/2-inch thick slices. Brown the slices under the broiler or in a toaster oven.

Caramelized Apricots

5 apricots, peeled, stoned and halved
3 tablespoons unsalted butter
3 tablespoons granulated sugar

Slice the apricots into wedges. In a pan over a medium-high heat, place the butter and sugar. Constantly stir the ingredients. When the sugar begins to brown, add the apricot slices. Brown the slices until they have a sugary coating. Cool the apricots.

Sugared Walnuts

1 cup chopped walnuts
1/4 cup granulated sugar
1 teaspoon salt
4 ounces Camembert

1. In a shallow pan, heat the walnuts over a medium-high heat. Stir the nuts frequently. When the nuts become brown and aromatic, increase the heat to high and sprinkle over the sugar and salt. Move the nuts around the pan until they are coated with sugar. Allow the nuts to cool.

2. Cut the Camembert into thin slices. Place a Camembert slice on a pumpernickel toast. Press one side of an apricot slice into the sugared walnuts. Place the apricot on the Camembert. Repeat this process with the remaining ingredients and serve.

Leek and Carrot Rolls Stuffed with Fennel and Comté Dressed with Champagne Vinaigrette

Champagne Vinaigrette

1 shallot, minced
1 teaspoon lemon juice
1 teaspoon salt
3 tablespoons champagne vinegar

1 garlic clove, minced
1 teaspoon lemon zest, minced
1/2 teaspoon freshly ground black pepper
1/2 cup extra-virgin olive oil

Whisk together the shallot, garlic, lemon juice, lemon zest, salt, pepper and vinegar. Gradually whisk in the olive oil. Set the vinaigrette aside.

Carrot and Leek Rolls Stuffed With Fennel and Comté

2 small heads of fennel
1 teaspoon salt
4 ounces Comté, cut 1/2-inch wide and 1/2-inch long
3 leeks

1 tablespoon olive oil
1/4 cup dry white wine

3 carrots, washed and peeled

1. Remove the dark green stalks and tough outer leaves from the fennel heads. Core the fennel and cut the leaves into 1/2-inch long matchsticks. In a shallow pan, place the olive oil over a medium-high heat. When the oil is hot, add the fennel and salt. Sauté the fennel until it has brown edges, about 10 minutes. Increase the heat to high and add the wine. Rapidly boil the wine until the pan is dry. Cool the fennel.

2. Cut the roots off of the leeks. Halve the leeks lengthwise and cut off any dark green ends. Separate the layers of the leeks and swirl them in a bowl of cold water until they are free of dirt. Plunge the leeks in a pot of boiling, salted water for 3 minutes. Strain the leeks and place them in a bowl of cold water to cool them completely. Dry the leeks on paper towels.

3. With a sharp knife or a mandoline, cut the carrots into long, paper thin slices. Plunge the slices into boiling, salted water for 5 minutes or until tender. Strain the carrot slices and place them in a bowl of ice water to cool them completely. Dry the carrots on paper towels.

4. Lay a leek strip flat. Top the leek with one or two carrot strips, depending on width. Place 1 piece of Comté and a few fennel strips on one of the shorter ends. Roll the leek and carrots around the cheese, forming a short, tight cylinder. Secure the roll with a toothpick. Repeat this process with the remaining leeks. Drizzle the vinaigrette over the rolls and serve them chilled.

Spinach Rolls with Basil, Mozzarella and Tomato Confit

Marinade

1/2 cup extra virgin olive oil
3 tablespoons balsamic vinegar
1 tablespoon raspberry vinegar
1 garlic clove, chopped
1 teaspoon Dijon mustard
Salt and pepper to taste

Combine all of the ingredients and whisk them thoroughly. Set the marinade aside.

Tomato Comfit

4 small, very ripe tomatoes
1/2 cup olive oil
1 shallot, chopped
2 garlic cloves, chopped
3 sprigs fresh thyme or 1/4 teaspoon dried

1. Preheat the oven to 275°F. Remove the cores from the tomatoes. With a knife, mark an X on the bottom of each tomato. Plunge the tomatoes in boiling water for 1 minute or until their skins begin to come off. Transfer the tomatoes to a bowl of ice water. When the tomatoes have cooled, remove the skins and cut each tomato into wedges. With a knife remove the seeds and membranes from the wedges, thus forming petal shapes.

2. Place the tomato petals in a roasting pan. Add the chopped shallots, garlic and thyme. Drizzle the olive oil over the tomatoes. Place the tomato petals in the oven and roast them for 30 minutes. Flip the tomato petals after 15 minutes.

3. Discard the thyme sprigs. Place the tomato petals on a grill to drain and cool.

Spinach leaves

1 pound large spinach leaves

1. Thoroughly wash the leaves in cold water to remove any sand. Firmly grasp the stem of a leaf and twist it, breaking the stem from the leaf without damaging the leaf. Remove the stems from the remaining spinach.

2. Plunge the spinach in boiling, salted water for 15 seconds. Transfer the leaves to a bowl of ice water. When the leaves have cooled completely, lay each leaf flat on paper towels to dry.

Basil Leaves and Mozzarella

1/2 cup fresh basil leaves
8 ounces mozzarella cheese

Wash the basil and remove any stems or buds. Slice the mozzarella into 1/4-inch thick matchsticks. Lay flat a large spinach leaf with its protruding veins facing upward. Top the large leaf with a smaller spinach leaf. Top the leaves with a tomato petal. Top the tomato with a basil leaf. Place a piece of mozzarella at the base of the spinach leaves. Beginning at the base, roll the spinach leaves, tomato and basil around the mozzarella. Pour the marinade over the spinach rolls and let them stand at room temperature for 30 minutes. Serve the rolls with toothpicks.

Cantaloupe and Papaya Slices with Goat Cheese on Carrot Nut Bread

Carrot Nut Bread

1 1/2 cup all purpose flour
3/4 teaspoon baking soda
1/4 teaspoon ground allspice
1/2 teaspoon ground ginger
2 tablespoons granulated sugar
1 egg, slightly beaten
1/4 cup vegetable oil
1/4 teaspoon salt
2 carrots, peeled and grated
3/4 cup chopped walnuts

Preheat the oven to 350°F. In a bowl, sift the flour, baking soda, cinnamon, allspice and ginger. Add the sugar, egg, oil and salt. Whisk the ingredients until they are completely incorporated. Fold the carrots and walnuts into the batter. Place the batter in a greased loaf pan and bake it for 45 minutes. Cool the bread on a grill. When the bread is completely cool, slice it into 1/4-inch slices.

Goat Cheese Spread

8 ounces goat cheese
1 tablespoon sour cream
2 tablespoons cream cheese
1 small cantaloupe, rind and seeds removed
2 papayas, peeled and seeded

1. With an electric beater, whip together the goat cheese, sour cream and cream cheese.

2. Thinly slice the cantaloupe and papaya. Spread 1 tablespoon of the goat cheese spread on a slice of carrot nut bread. Top the spread with a few slices of the cantaloupe and papaya. Repeat this process with the remaining cantaloupe and papaya. Serve the canapés at room temperature.

Glazed Radishes with Black Bean Purée

Makes 35 Canapés

Black Bean Purée

1 cup dried black beans
1 Serrano chili, core, seeds and membranes removed
2 shallots, finely chopped
1 carrot, peeled and chopped
2 garlic cloves, peeled and chopped
1/2 teaspoon ground cardamom
1 tablespoon ground ginger
1 tablespoon chili powder
1 teaspoon black pepper
1 teaspoon salt
2 tablespoons plain yogurt
2 tablespoons lemon juice
2 tablespoons fresh oregano leaves
2 tablespoons fresh parsley leaves
1 tablespoon tahini

1. Cover the beans with water and soak overnight.

2. Drain the beans and pick out any stones. Coarsely chop the serrano chili. In a pot, place the serrano chili, black beans, shallots, carrots, garlic, cardamom, ginger and chili powder. Fill the pot with enough water to cover the beans by 2 inches. Place the pot over a high heat. When the beans boil, reduce the heat to medium and lightly simmer the beans for 3—3 1/2 hours or until they are tender, adding water as needed. Strain the beans and reserve 3 tablespoons of the cooking liquid.

3. Working in batches, place the beans, pepper, salt, yogurt, lemon juice, oregano, parsley, tahini and the reserved cooking liquid in a blender or food processor. Blend the ingredients until they are smooth. Chill the purée.

Glazed Radishes

35 small radishes
1 tablespoon unsalted butter
1 teaspoon granulated sugar
1 tablespoon salt

1. Remove the greens from the radishes. Wash and scrub the radishes. Place the radishes, butter, sugar and salt in a deep pan. Fill the pan with enough water to cover the radishes. Place the pan over a high heat. When the water boils, partially cover the radishes and reduce the heat to medium. Continue to simmer the radishes until most of the water has evaporated. Cool the radishes.

2. With a sharp paring knife or a melon baller, hollow out the center of each radish. Cut thin slices off of the bottoms of the radishes to help them stand flat.

3. Place the Black Bean Purée in a pastry bag. Pipe the purée into the radishes. Serve the radishes chilled.

Red Cabbage Chiffonade with Apple Chutney and Walnuts on Herb Toasts

Makes 40 Canapés

Herb Toasts

2 1/2 cups all purpose flour
1 teaspoon salt
1 cup water
1 beaten egg
1 teaspoon ground cumin seed
cornmeal

2 tablespoons granulated sugar
1 teaspoon dry active yeast
2 tablespoons shortening or lard
1 teaspoon ground ginger
1 teaspoon celery seed

1. In a bowl, combine 1 1/4 cups of the flour, the sugar, salt and yeast. In a small pot over a medium heat, place the water and shortening. When the shortening has melted, gradually add it to the flour. Stir in the egg, spices and 1/4 cup of the flour to the batter. Gradually stir in the remaining flour, until the dough comes off of the sides of the bowl.

2. On a floured surface, knead the dough for 10 minutes or until it is smooth and elastic. Place the dough in an oiled bowl and flip it to oil all sides. Allow the dough to rise in a warm, draft free area, until it has doubled in bulk. Shape the dough into 2 loaves. Generously sprinkle cornmeal onto a baking sheet. Place the loaves, seam sides down on the baking sheet. Cover the loaves and allow them to rise in a draft free area, until they have doubled in size. Place the loaves in a cold oven and set the heat at 400°. After 15 minutes, reduce the heat to 375° and allow the loaves to bake for an additional 25 minutes. Cool the loaves on a grill.

3. Preheat the broiler. Thinly slice the loaves. Toast the slices under the broiler until they are golden brown.

Red Cabbage Chiffonade

1/2 small red cabbage
2 quarts boiling water
1 tablespoon fresh ginger, peeled and coarsely chopped
2 garlic cloves, peeled and chopped
1 tablespoon apple cider vinegar
1/2 cup olive oil

1 cup red wine vinegar
1 shallot, coarsely chopped

1 tablespoon lemon zest, finely chopped
3 tablespoons raspberry vinegar
2 tablespoons sesame oil

1. Halve the cabbage and remove the core. Cut the cabbage into very thin, long strips. Wash the cabbage and place it in a heat proof bowl. Heat the red wine vinegar and pour it over the cabbage. The vinegar will keep the cabbage a brilliant magenta. Pour the boiling water over the cabbage and let it sit for 4 minutes. Strain the cabbage.

2. Whisk together the remaining ingredients and pour them over the cabbage. Toss the cabbage well and allow it to marinate for 1 hour.

Apple Chutney

1/2 cup granulated sugar	1 tablespoon lemon juice
1/2 cup red wine	1/2 cup orange juice
3 Granny Smith apples, peeled, cored and finely chopped	
2 whole cloves	1 teaspoon ground allspice
1 teaspoon cinnamon	1 cup water
1/2 cup finely chopped walnuts	

1. Place 1/2 cup of water with the sugar and lemon juice in a pot over a high heat. When the sugar turns a deep amber, add the red wine {be very careful of the steam}. Simmer this mixture until it is syrupy. Add the orange juice, cloves, allspice and cinnamon and reduce the heat to medium. Add the apples and remaining water to the pot. Simmer the ingredients for 30 minutes or until the apples are tender. Remove the cloves and discard them. Cool the chutney completely.

2. Preheat the oven to 400°F. Spread the walnuts evenly on a cookie sheet. Place the cookie sheet in the oven. Roast the nuts until they are slightly browned and aromatic, about 5 minutes. Take the cookie sheet out of the oven and transfer the nuts to a plate. While the nuts are on the hot cookie sheet they will continue to cook.

3. Place a mound of cabbage on a toast. Top the cabbage with a spoonful of apple chutney. Sprinkle chopped walnuts on top. Repeat this process with the remaining ingredients.

Fish

I was raised sailing and loving the water. In the Caribbean, I have noticed that Mahi Mahi is commonly featured as the Chef's Special of the Day. During an interview with a fisherman, I inquired why Mahi Mahi is such a popular special. "That's easy," he replied with grin, "Mahi Mahi means what washed up on the beach this morning."

Anchovy Wrapped Capers with Mozzarella and Olive Tapenade on Zucchini Slices

Makes 24 Canapés

You may serve these on toasted bread as well.

Tapenade

1 cup Kalamata olives, pitted
1 tablespoon lemon juice
2 garlic cloves, peeled and chopped
1 tablespoon extra virgin olive oil

Place the olives, lemon juice and garlic in a food processor. Blend the ingredients until they are smooth. With the machine running, gradually add the olive oil.

Anchovy Wrapped Capers

24 anchovy filets
1 cup milk
24 large capers
6 ounces fresh mozzarella, sliced into thin rounds
3 large zucchini

1. Place the anchovies in the milk. Allow the anchovies to soak for 1 hour. This alleviates most of the saltiness. Slice the zucchini, on the bias, into thick slices.

2. Strain the anchovies in a colander and discard the milk. Lay an anchovy filet flat on a clean work surface. Place a caper on one end of the filet and roll the anchovy around the caper.

3. Spread 1 teaspoon of tapenade on the zucchini. Top the tapenade with a mozzarella slice. Top the mozzarella with an anchovy wrapped caper. Serve the canapés chilled.

Smoked Trout and Tomato Quiches

Makes 35 Quiches

Smoked Trout

If you do not own a smoker, you local fish shop will have prepackaged smoked trout.

2 tablespoons soy sauce
1 tablespoon rice wine vinegar
2 tablespoons brown sugar
1/4 cup fresh cilantro leaves, finely chopped
2 garlic cloves, finely chopped
1 tablespoon fresh ginger, peeled and finely chopped
2 tablespoons lemon juice
2 tablespoons sesame oil
3 tablespoons extra virgin olive oil
1 pound trout filets
Alder wood chips

1. Whisk together all of the ingredients except for the trout and wood chips. Pour the marinade over the trout and refrigerate the filets for 4-6 hours.

2. Prepare the smoker with Alder wood chips. Drain the trout filets and hot smoke them at 110°F for 20 minutes. Cool the trout filets. Remove the skins from the filets and flake the trout flesh. Refrigerate the trout.

Quiche Shells

1/4 cup cold unsalted butter, cut into small pieces
3/4 cup all purpose flour
1/2 teaspoon salt
1 large egg, beaten
1 teaspoon water
2 tablespoons fennel seed

1. Combine the butter, salt and flour. Rub these ingredients between one's hands or pulse them in a food processor until they form a coarse meal. Gradually add the egg, water and fennel seeds until a firm dough forms. Wrap the dough in plastic and refrigerate it for 30 minutes.

2. Preheat the oven to 325°F. Generously butter a muffin pan. Dust the muffin pan with

flour and refrigerate it. On a lightly floured surface, roll the dough 1/4-inch thick. Cut rounds out of the dough and place them in the muffin tins. Insure that there is no air between the crust and the pan. Prick holes in the dough with a fork. Decoratively crimp the crusts of the quiche shells.

Chill the crusts for 30 minutes. Line the quiche shells with parchment paper. Fill the shells with beans. Bake the shells for 5 minutes. Remove the beans and continue to cook the shells for 3 minutes or until they are just beginning to brown. Cool the shells.

Tomatoes

2 tomatoes

Core the tomatoes. With a paring knife, mark the bottom of each tomato with an X. Plunge the tomatoes in a pot of boiling water for 1 minute, or until the skins begin to come off. Transfer the tomatoes to a bowl of ice water. When they have cooled completely, peel the skins off of the tomatoes. Halve the tomatoes widthwise. Remove the seeds and coarsely chop the tomatoes.

Celery

3 celery stalks
1 tablespoon olive oil

Wash the celery and remove any leaves. Finely chop the celery. Place the olive oil in a pan over a medium-high heat. When the oil is hot, add the celery. Sauté the celery until it is translucent, about 10 minutes. Drain and cool the celery.

Quiche Custard

1 cup heavy cream
2 large eggs
1 teaspoon salt
1/2 teaspoon white pepper
4 ounces goat cheese

Preheat the oven to 325°F. Whisk together the cream, eggs, salt and pepper. Place one tablespoon of the celery and the tomato in the bottom of the shell. Place 1 teaspoon of goat cheese in the shell and top it with a few trout flakes. Pour the custard to 3/4 of the height of the shell. Repeat with the remaining shells. Bake the quiches for 10 minutes or until an inserted toothpick comes out clean.

Trout with Avocado Purée on Sesame Crackers

Makes 35 Canapés

Sesame Crackers

1/4 teaspoon dry active yeast
1/4 cup warm water, 105-115°F
1 teaspoon salt
1 egg, beaten with 2 tablespoons water

1/2 teaspoon granulated sugar
1 1/2 cups all purpose flour
1/4 cup milk
1/4 cup white sesame seeds, lightly toasted

1. Sprinkle the yeast and sugar over the warm water. Stir the water until the yeast has dissolved. Place the yeast in a warm, draft free place. Allow the yeast mixture to rise until it is foamy, about 10 minutes.

2. In a separate bowl, combine the flour and salt and form them into a well. Add to the center of the well the yeast mixture and the milk. Gradually combine the wet and dry ingredients until a smooth dough has formed. On a lightly floured surface, knead the dough for 10 minutes or until it is elastic. Place the dough in a greased bowl and flip it to oil all sides. Cover the dough with plastic wrap. Place the dough in a warm place and let it rise until it has doubled in bulk, about 2-3 hours.

3. Gently deflate the dough and divide it into 6 portions. Cover the dough and let it rise for 30 minutes.

4. Preheat the oven to 400°F. On a lightly floured surface, roll the portions of dough into 1/8th-inch thick rounds. Brush the rounds with the beaten egg and water. Sprinkle the rounds with toasted sesame seeds. With a knife, cut the rounds into triangles. Working in batches if necessary, transfer the triangles to a greased cookie sheet. Top the triangles with a grate. Bake the triangles for 5-7 minutes or until they are crisp. Cool the crackers on a grill.

Trout Marinade

1/4 cup yellow onion, finely chopped
1 teaspoon Chinese five spices
Juice of 1 lime
1/4 cup sesame oil
1 tablespoon fresh ginger, peeled and chopped

1/4 cup soy sauce
4 cilantro stems
Zest of 1 lime, chopped
2 pounds trout filets

1. Whisk together the onion, soy sauce, Chinese five spices, cilantro stems, lime juice, lime zest, ginger and sesame oil. Pour the marinade over the trout, refrigerate and let it marinate for 4 hours.

2. Preheat the oven to 350°F. Remove the trout from the marinade. Place the trout, skin side down in a roasting pan. Bake the trout for 10 minutes or until it is just cooked through. Remove trout from the oven and cool it.

3. Remove the skin from the trout and flake each filet into 1-inch pieces. Set the trout aside.

Radish Dice

2 purple radishes, peeled and diced finely 1 shallot, finely chopped
1 cup water 2 tablespoons flat leaf parsley leaves, finely chopped

In a shallow pan over a medium-high heat, combine the radishes, shallot and water. Simmer the radishes until they are soft, about 15 minutes. Add the chopped parsley and set the radishes aside to cool.

Shiitake Slices

2 cups shiitake mushrooms, cleaned 1 tablespoon olive oil
3 green onions, finely chopped 1 tablespoon fresh ginger, peeled and finely chopped

Remove the stems from the shiitakes. Finely slice the shiitakes. Heat the olive oil in a pan over a medium-high heat. When the oil is hot, add the shiitakes and sauté them for 5 minutes. Add the green onions and ginger to the mushrooms. Continue to sauté the mushrooms until they are limp and shiny. Strain the mushrooms and reserve any liquid for the avocado purée.

Avocado Purée

1 Haas avocado, peeled and deseeded 1/4 cup fresh cilantro leaves
Reserved cooking liquid from the shiitake mushrooms

1. In a blender or food processor, combine the avocado, cilantro and mushroom liquid. Blend the ingredients until the mixture is smooth.

2. On a sesame chip, place 1 tablespoon of radish dice. Place some shiitake slices on the radishes. Top the mushrooms with a piece of trout and a squirt of avocado purée. Repeat this process with the remaining trout pieces. Serve the canapés warm or chilled.

Catfish Nuggets with Raspberry Dipping Sauce

Makes 35 Canapés

Raspberry Dipping Sauce

4 medium sized beets
2 tablespoons red wine vinegar
1/4 cup granulated sugar
8 ounces frozen raspberries
1 rosemary sprig

1. Remove the greens from the beets. Scrub the beets under cold, running water. Place the beets in a pot of boiling, salted water and cover them. Reduce the heat to medium-high and simmer the beets for 40 minutes or until they are tender. Peel the beets under running water and coarsely chop them.

2. In a pot over a medium heat, place the raspberries, vinegar, rosemary and sugar. Lightly simmer the raspberries for 20 minutes or until they no longer hold their form. Strain the raspberries through a fine sieve. Place the raspberry juice and beets in a blender or food processor. Blend the beets until they are smooth. Set the sauce aside.

Fried Catfish

1 1/2 pounds Catfish filets
1/4 cup cornmeal
1 teaspoon ground cumin seed
1 teaspoon salt
1 cup all purpose flour
3 cups canola oil
1 1/2 cups cracker crumbs, finely ground
1 teaspoon chili powder
1 teaspoon curry powder
1 teaspoon white pepper
2 eggs beaten with 2 tablespoons water

1. Cut the catfish filets into 1-inch long and 1/4-inch wide strips. Combine the cracker crumbs, cornmeal, chili powder, cumin, curry, salt and pepper. Dredge the strips in the flour. Transfer the strips to the egg and water mixture. Wipe any excess egg off of the catfish strips and dredge them in the cracker crumb mixture.

2. In a pot, heat the oil over a medium-high heat to 350°F. Test the oil's heat by adding one of the catfish strips. If the strip bubbles, then the oil is hot. Working in batches, fry the strips for 5-7 minutes or until they are golden brown and cooked through. Remove any excess grease by patting the strips with paper towels. Serve the strips warm with the raspberry dipping sauce on the side.

Catfish and Basil Sausage with Cantaloupe Sauce on Sesame Pita Chips

Sesame Pita Chips

1 teaspoon dry active yeast
1 teaspoon sesame oil
1/2 cup warm water, 105-115°F
1 teaspoon honey
2 tablespoons sesame seeds
1 1/2 cups bread flour
1/2 teaspoon salt

1. Whisk together the yeast, sesame oil, warm water and honey. In a separate bowl, combine the sesame seeds, flour and salt and add them to the yeast mixture. Stir the mixture with a wooden spoon until a firm dough forms. On a floured surface, knead the dough until it is smooth and elastic, about 10 minutes. Place the dough in an oiled bowl and flip it to oil all sides. Cover the bowl with a towel and place it in a warm place. Allow the dough to rise until it has doubled in bulk.

2. Gently deflate the dough and divide it into 5 portions. Let the portions rest for 10 minutes.

3. Preheat the oven to 500°F. Place a baking sheet in the oven. Working with one's palm on a floured surface, form each portion of dough into a 1/4-inch thick round. Rest the rounds for 10 minutes. Place the rounds on the heated baking sheet and bake them until they puff up and brown, about 3 minutes on each side.

4. Peel the two layers of each pita in half to form 2 separate rounds. Cut the rounds into triangles. Toast the triangles until crisp.

Cantaloupe Sauce

1/2 cantaloupe
2 tablespoons lemon juice
2 tablespoons lime juice

Remove the seeds and rind from the cantaloupe. Chop the cantaloupe and place it in a blender with the lemon and lime juices. Blend the cantaloupe until it is smooth. Chill the sauce.

Catfish and Basil Sausages

1 pound catfish filets
3 egg yolks, very cold
1 teaspoon salt
1 teaspoon white pepper
1/4 cup heavy cream, very cold
1/4 cup fresh basil leaves, chopped
4 ounces sausage casings
3 cups fish stock or water
1 tablespoon unsalted butter

1. Place the bowl and blade of a food processor in the freezer for 30 minutes prior to use. Use the chilled bowl and blade to purée the catfish filets. With the machine running, add the egg yolks, salt, pepper, cream and basil. When the ingredients are completely incorporated place the sausage in a pastry bag and refrigerate it.

2. Wash the sausage casings. Run a bit of water through the casings to insure there are no holes. Tie a knot at the end of one of the casings and pipe the sausage into the casing. With a small knife, prick the sides of the sausage. Alternatively you can make quenelles out of the sausage.

3. In a shallow pot, place the fish stock. Place the pot over a medium-high heat. When the stock simmers, add the sausage and reduce the heat to medium. Poach the sausage for 3 minutes on each side. Remove the sausage from the pot and pat it dry.

4. Heat the butter over a medium-high heat. When the butter foams add the sausage. Brown the sausage on both sides. Remove the sausage from the pan and thickly slice it.

5. Spread a teaspoon of cantaloupe sauce on a pita chip. Top with a slice of sausage. Repeat this process with the remaining sausage. Serve the canapés warm or chilled.

Cured Salmon with Fennel Cream on Cucumber Slices

Cured Salmon

1 1/2 pound salmon filets
1/4 cup kosher salt
1 cup fennel stems, chopped
1/4 cup light brown sugar
Zest of 2 lemons

1. Cut the salmon in half lengthwise. In a bowl, combine the brown sugar, kosher salt and lemon zest. Cover the filet halves with the brown sugar mixture and the chopped fennel stems. Place one half of the salmon on the other half with the flesh sides against each other. Place the filets in a colander over a bowl. Weight the filets with a plate and a one pound can. Chill the filets for 8-10 hours. Flip the fillets and chill them for an additional 8-10 hours.

2. Wipe off the brown sugar mixture. With a very sharp knife, slice the salmon very thinly. If you're having trouble slicing the salmon, put it in the freezer for 15 minutes. This will firm up the flesh and make slicing easier. Refrigerate the salmon slices.

Fennel Cream

2 heads fennel
3 tablespoons rice wine vinegar
1 cup cream cheese, softened
1 small red onion
2 tablespoons lime juice

1. Remove the coarse outer leaves of the fennel heads. Core the fennel heads and finely chop them. Plunge the fennel in boiling, salted water for 7 minutes or until it is tender. Drain and cool the fennel.

2. Finely chop the red onion. Whisk together the onion, fennel, rice wine vinegar, lime juice and cream cheese. Chill the fennel cream.

Cucumber Slices

2 large cucumbers

1. Cut the cucumbers into thick slices. Lightly salt the slices and drain them in a colander for 10 minutes.

2. Spread 1 teaspoon of the fennel cream on each of the cucumber slices. Top the fennel cream with one of the salmon slices. Garnish the canapés with fennel sprigs. Serve the canapés chilled.

Smoked Salmon Cakes with Jalapeño Tartar

Smoked Salmon Cakes

Alder wood chips
2 celery stalks, finely chopped
3 scallions, finely chopped
3 tablespoons mayonnaise
2 teaspoons salt
1/4 cup fresh cilantro leaves, finely chopped
1 Anaheim chili, cored, seeded and finely chopped
5 tablespoons olive oil

1 pound salmon filet
1 carrot, peeled and finely chopped
1 egg, slightly beaten
1 3/4 cups cracker crumbs, finely ground
1 teaspoon white pepper

1. Prepare the smoker with alder wood chips. Hot smoke the salmon for 10 minutes or until it is just cooked through. Prepare the tartar while the salmon is cooling.

2. With a fork, flake the salmon and place it in a mixing bowl. Add to the salmon, the celery, carrot, Anaheim chili, scallions, cilantro, egg, mayonnaise, 1/2 cup of the cracker crumbs, salt and pepper. Mix the ingredients until they are completely incorporated. Form small patties out of 2 tablespoons of the salmon mixture. Refrigerate the patties for 30 minutes. Dredge the patties in the remaining cracker crumbs and refrigerate them for an additional 15 minutes.

3. Place 1 tablespoon of the olive oil in a shallow pan over a medium-high heat. When the oil is hot, add a few of the patties and fry them for 4-6 minutes on each side. Transfer the patties to paper towels to remove any excess grease. Repeat this process with the remaining patties.

Jalapeño Tartar

1/2 cup canned jalapeños
2 tablespoons canned jalapeño liquid
1/2 yellow onion, finely chopped
2 tablespoons curly parsley, finely chopped
2 cups mayonnaise

1. In a food processor, combine all of the ingredients and serve the sauce chilled with the warm salmon cakes.

Spinach, Carrot and Beet Terrine of Sole with Cumin Sesame Crackers

Cumin Sesame Crackers

1/2 teaspoon dry active yeast
1 tablespoon honey
2 tablespoons water
1 cup all purpose flour
4 tablespoons cumin seeds

2 tablespoons warm water, 105-115°F
1 tablespoon whipping cream
1 teaspoon unsalted butter, melted
1 teaspoon salt
Kosher salt

1. Sprinkle the yeast over the warm water. Add the honey to the yeast mixture. Place the yeast mixture in a warm, draft free area until it is foamy, about 10 minutes.

2. In a pot, place the whipping cream, water and melted butter. Heat this mixture over a medium heat. When the liquids are 105-115°F, transfer them to a bowl. Whisk the yeast mixture into the cream mixture. In a separate bowl, combine the flour and salt. Add 1/2 cup of the flour and salt to the yeast and cream mixture. Whisk the mixture firmly until it is smooth. Add the remaining flour 1/4 cup at a time, until a shaggy dough forms.

3. Turn the dough out onto a floured surface and knead it for 10 minutes or until it is smooth and elastic. Place the dough in a greased bowl and flip it to grease all sides. Let the dough rise in a warm place until it has doubled in size.

4. Place a pan over a high heat. When the pan is hot, add the cumin seeds. Toast the seeds until they are aromatic. Cool the seeds.

5. Preheat the oven to 350°F. On a floured surface, gently deflate the dough and knead it for 5 minutes. Split the dough into 4 portions. Knead equal amounts of the cooled seeds into each portion of the dough. Roll a portion of the dough paper thin or pass it through a pasta machine. Place the dough on a well greased baking sheet and sprinkle it with kosher salt. Cover the dough with a grill. Bake each portion of dough for 10-15 minutes or until they are golden. Repeat this process with the other portions. Cool the cracker on a grill. Cut or break the cracker into 2-inch squares. For uniform crackers, make shapes of the dough before baking with a cookie cutter or knife.

Roasted Beets

5 beets

1. Preheat the oven to 400°F. Remove the greens from the beets. Delicately scrub the beets under cold water until they are free of dirt. Dry the beets and place them in a roasting pan. Place the beets in the oven and roast them for 45 minutes to an hour. When the skins of the beets are ballooning, the beets have finished cooking. Let the beets stand until they are cool enough to handle.

2. Under cold, running water remove the skins from the beets. Coarsely chop the beets and purée them in a blender or food processor with 1/4 cup of water. Strain the beets and chill the juice.

Carrots

3 carrots
1 teaspoon granulated sugar
1/2 teaspoon salt
1 thyme sprig
1 tablespoon unsalted butter

1. Peel and slice the carrots. Place the carrots in a pan with the thyme, sugar, butter and salt. Fill the pan with water to the height of the carrots. Leaving a small opening for steam to escape, cover the carrots and place them over a medium heat.

2. When carrots are tender, remove the thyme. Purée the carrots in a food processor or blender. Strain the carrots through a fine sieve and chill the juice.

Spinach

4 cups spinach
1 tablespoon unsalted butter

1. Destem the spinach and wash it thoroughly in cold water. Place half of the butter in a pan and melt it over a medium-high heat. Working in batches, add the spinach to the pan and sauté it until the leaves are wilted. Repeat this process with the remaining spinach.

2. Strain the spinach in a colander and squeeze out any excess water. Purée the leaves in a food processor or blender. Chill the spinach purée.

Sole mousse

1 pound sole filets
2 egg whites
1 cup very cold heavy cream
1 teaspoon salt
1/2 teaspoon cayenne pepper

1. Place the food processor bowl and blade in the freezer for thirty minutes prior to use.

2. Coarsely chop the sole and purée it in the food processor until it is smooth. With the machine running, add the egg whites. When the egg whites and sole are combined, gradually add the cream and then the salt and pepper.

2. Divide the mousse into 3 portions. While working with one portion refrigerate the remaining portions. Add the carrot juice to one of the thirds, the beet juice to another third and the chopped spinach to the remaining third.

3. Preheat the oven to 325°F. With a pastry bag, line a well buttered terrine mold with equal layers of beet, spinach and carrot mousse. Drop the mold from 1-inch high to pop any air bubbles. Cover the mold with well buttered, oven safe paper.

4. Place 2 layers of paper towels on the bottom of a roasting pan. Place the covered mold in the pan and put the pan in the oven. Fill the roasting pan with boiling water to 2/3rds the height of the mold. Cook the terrine for 25 minutes. Test doneness by placing a knife or metal skewer in the center of the terrine. When the knife comes out clean, the terrine is finished.

5. Chill the terrine in the mold for at least 2 hours. Run a knife along the sides of the mold to unstick the terrine. On a flat surface, turn the mold over. Serve the mousse chilled with the cumin sesame crackers on the side.

Poached Halibut with Tarragon Sauce and Lettuce Leaves on Walnut Toasts

Makes 35 Canapés

Walnut Toasts

1 teaspoon honey
1 teaspoon dry active yeast
1/2 teaspoon ground allspice
1 teaspoon salt
1/4 cup walnuts, finely chopped

2 tablespoons warm water, 105-115°F
1/3 cup milk
2 tablespoons unsalted butter
1 1/2 cups all purpose flour

1. Combine the honey and warm water. Sprinkle the yeast over the water. Allow the yeast to rise in a warm, draft free area, until it is foamy, about 10 minutes.

2. Place in a pot over a low heat, the milk, allspice and butter. When the butter has melted, remove the pot from the heat. When the milk mixture is lukewarm, add it to the yeast mixture. In a separate bowl, combine the salt and flour. Gradually add the flour to the yeast mixture until a shaggy dough forms. On a floured surface, knead the dough until it is smooth and elastic, about 10 minutes. Place the dough in an oiled bowl and flip it to oil all sides. Cover the dough and place it in a warm, draft free area. Allow the dough to rise until it has doubled in bulk.

3. Preheat the oven to 375°F. Gently deflate the dough and knead in the walnuts. Divide the dough into two. Place each half of the dough in a well buttered loaf tin. Cover the loaves and allow them to rise in a warm, draft free area until they have doubled in bulk.

4. Bake the loaves for 25-30 minutes or until a toothpick comes out clean. Cool the loaves on a grill. Preheat the broiler. Cut the loaf into 1/2 -thick slices. Toast the slices until golden brown.

Poached Halibut

2 quarts water
1 shallot, chopped
2 celery stalks, chopped
5 peppercorns
1/2 cup dry white wine
1 1/2 pounds halibut filet

1. In a pot, combine the water, shallot, celery, peppercorns and wine. Place the pot over a high heat. When the liquid boils, reduce the heat to medium. Simmer the poaching liquid for 15 minutes.

2. Slice the halibut into bite size pieces. Place the halibut pieces in the poaching liquid. Poach the halibut pieces for 4-5 minutes or until they are cooked through. Remove the halibut pieces from the liquid and dry them completely.

3. Strain the poaching liquid into a sauce pan. Increase the heat of the poaching liquid to high and reduce the liquid until only one cup remains.

Tarragon Sauce

1 cup poaching liquid
1 tablespoon Dijon mustard
1/2 cup heavy cream
1 teaspoon salt
1/4 cup fresh tarragon leaves, finely chopped
2 cups red lettuce leaves, torn into bite size pieces

1. In a pot over medium-high heat, whisk together the poaching liquid, mustard and cream. Reduce this liquid for 10 minutes or until it is thick enough to coat a spoon. Add the salt and tarragon to the sauce. Keep the sauce warm.

2. Place a lettuce leaf on a slice of walnut bread. Top the lettuce with a piece of halibut. Top the halibut with 1 teaspoon of the sauce. Repeat this process with the remaining pieces of halibut. Serve the canapés warm or chilled.

Potato Crusted Halibut with Fennel Relish on Sour Cream Toasts

Makes 40 Canapés

Sour Cream Toasts

1 tablespoon dry active yeast
1/4 cup warm water, 105-115°F
1/4 teaspoon baking soda
2 1/2 cups all purpose flour

1 teaspoon granulated sugar
3/4 cup sour cream, room temperature
1 tablespoon salt
Cornmeal

1. Sprinkle the yeast and sugar over the warm water. Place the yeast mixture in a warm, draft-free area until it is foamy, about 10 minutes.

2. Combine the sour cream and baking soda. Add this mixture to the yeast. In a separate bowl, combine the salt and flour. Gradually add the flour to the yeast. Mix the ingredients until a firm dough forms. On a floured surface, knead the dough until it is elastic and smooth, about 10 minutes. Place the dough in an oiled bowl and flip it to oil all sides. Cover the dough and place it in a warm area until it has doubled in bulk.

3. Preheat the oven to 375°F. Generously sprinkle cornmeal on a baking sheet. Gently deflate the dough and halve it. Pull one half of the dough into a rectangle. Beginning on one of the wider ends, roll the rectangle into a long, cylindrical loaf. Repeat with the other half. Place the loaves, seam-sides down, on the baking sheet. Cover the loaves and place them in a warm area, until they have doubled in bulk.

4. Bake the loaves for 25-30 minutes. Cool the loaves on a grill. Preheat the broiler. Thinly slice the loaves. Toast the slices under the broiler until they are slightly brown.

Fennel Relish

2 small fennel heads
1 teaspoon salt
1/2 small red onion, finely chopped
1 tablespoon olive oil
1/2 cup sweet white wine
1 teaspoon black pepper, freshly ground

Cut the stalks off of the fennel heads and remove the tough outer leaves. Core the fennel heads and chop them finely. Place the olive oil in a shallow pan over a medium-high heat. When the oil is hot, add the chopped fennel and salt to the pan. Sauté the fennel until it is soft, about 10 minutes. Increase the heat to high and add the wine. When the wine has reduced completely, remove the pan from the heat. Place the fennel in a mixing bowl and add the red onion and pepper.

Potato Crusted Halibut

1 small russet potato
2 pounds halibut filet
salt and pepper
1/4 cup olive oil

1. Wash and peel the potato. Using a vegetable slicer, thinly slice the potato into strips or strands. Place the strips in a bowl of water.

2. Slice the halibut into bite-size pieces. Lightly salt and pepper the pieces. Squeeze the water out of the potato strands. Place some potato strands on the top of each piece of halibut. In a shallow pan, heat the olive oil over a medium-high heat. There should be enough oil to completely encase the potato strips. When the oil is hot, place a few pieces of halibut, potato-sides down, in the pan. Fry the halibut for 3-5 minutes or until the potatoes are golden brown. Flip the halibut and fry the other side for 2-5 minutes, depending on the thickness of your fish.

3. Place one tablespoon of fennel relish on a sour cream toast. Top the relish with a piece of halibut. Repeat this process with the remaining pieces of halibut. Serve the canapés warm.

Prosciutto Stuffed Halibut with Radicchio on Cornmeal Toasts

Makes 40 Canapés

Cornmeal Toasts

1/4 cup cornmeal
2 teaspoons salt
1/2 teaspoon granulated sugar
2 tablespoons light brown sugar
2 1/2 cups all-purpose flour

3/4 cup water, 105-115°F
1 teaspoon dry active yeast
1/4 cup warm milk, 105-115°F
1 teaspoon ground allspice

1. In a small pot over a medium-high heat, combine the cornmeal, 1/4 cup of the water and 1/2 teaspoon of the salt. Stir this mixture until it is thick, about 4 minutes. Transfer to a bowl and set aside to cool.

2. Sprinkle the yeast and sugar over the remaining warm water. Allow the yeast to rise in a warm, draft-free area until it is foamy, about 10 minutes. Combine the cornmeal and yeast mixtures. Add the milk, brown sugar, allspice and the remaining salt. While stirring, gradually add the flour until a shaggy dough forms. On a floured surface, knead the dough until it is smooth and elastic, about 10 minutes. Place the dough in an oiled bowl and flip it to oil all sides. Cover the dough and allow it to rise in a warm, draft-free area until it has doubled in bulk.

4. Preheat the oven to 425°F. Generously sprinkle cornmeal on a baking sheet. Gently deflate the dough and halve it. Stretch each half into a rectangle. Beginning with one of the longer sides, roll the dough into a loaf. Repeat with the other rectangle and place the loaves seam-sides down on the baking sheet. Cover the loaves and allow them to rise in a warm place until they have doubled in bulk.

5. Bake the loaves 10 minutes and then reduce the heat to 350°F. Bake the loaves for an additional 20-25 minutes. Cool the loaves completely and cut them into 1/2-inch slices. Toast the slices under the broiler.

Prosciutto Stuffed Halibut

1 1/2 pounds halibut filet
8 prosciutto slices
1/2 cup fresh sage leaves
1 teaspoon black pepper
1/3 cup raspberry vinegar
1 cup + 2 tablespoons olive oil
2 radicchio heads, washed, cored and coarsely chopped
salt and pepper

1. Place the halibut filet on a flat surface, skin-side down. Cover the filet with plastic wrap. With the smooth side of a mallet or a small pot, pound the halibut until it is 1/4-inch thick. Remove the plastic wrap and place the prosciutto slices on top of the filet. Top the prosciutto with sage leaves. Starting at one of the wide edges, tightly roll the fillet into a cylinder. Roll wax paper around the cylinder and freeze it for 30 minutes.

2. Combine the pepper, raspberry vinegar and 3/4 tablespoons of the olive oil and pour it over the radicchio.

3. Take the halibut out of the freezer. Cut 1/4-inch slices off of the roll. Lightly salt and pepper the slices. In a shallow pan, heat 1 tablespoon of olive oil. When the oil is hot, place the halibut slices in the pan. Work in batches as not to crowd the fish. Brown the slices for 4 minutes on each side, or until cooked through. Remove the slices from the pan and slice them in half to form half-moons.

4. Place a bit of radicchio on a cornmeal toast. Top the radicchio with a half-moon slice. Repeat this process with the remaining half-moons. Serve the canapés warm or chilled.

Spicy Tuna with Carrot and Cucumber Slaw on Chapati Crisps

Makes 35 Canapés

Chapati Crisps

2 cups whole wheat flour
1/2 cup lukewarm water
1 tablespoon vegetable oil

1. In a bowl, form a well out of the flour. Fill the middle of the well with the water. Gradually combine the flour and the water until a firm dough forms. Knead the dough on a lightly floured surface for 10 minutes or until it is smooth and elastic. Place the dough in a greased bowl. Flip the dough to oil all sides. Place a damp cloth over the bowl and allow the dough to rise in a warm place for 1 hour.

2. Divide the dough into 8 portions. Roll each portion into a 1/4-inch thick round. Stretch each round by slapping it from one hand to the other.

3. Preheat the broiler. Place a skillet over a high heat. When the skillet is hot, place a round on it. Cook the rounds for 1-2 minutes on each side or until they are bubbly and brown. Repeat this process with the remaining portions of dough. Cut the rounds into triangles. Toast the triangles under the broiler until they are crisp.

Carrot and Cucumber Slaw

2 carrots
2 cucumbers, peeled and deseeded
2 tablespoons rice wine vinegar
1 teaspoon freshly ground black pepper
1 teaspoon fresh ginger, peeled and minced

Peel the carrots and cut them into toothpick-sized strips. Cut the cucumbers into toothpick-sized strips. Pour the rice wine vinegar over the vegetables. Add the freshly ground pepper and ginger to the vegetables and toss them to coat. Refrigerate the slaw.

Spicy Tuna

1 1/2 pounds Yellow Fin Tuna filet, sushi grade
4 green onions, finely sliced
1/4 cup fresh cilantro leaves, finely chopped
1 teaspoon fresh ginger, peeled and finely chopped
1 garlic clove, finely chopped
Juice of 1 lime
1 teaspoon green chili paste
1 teaspoon Dijon mustard
1/4 cup soy sauce
1 tablespoon sesame oil

1. Cut the tuna into small cubes. Whisk together the remaining ingredients. Toss the tuna in the dressing.

2. Place a bed of carrot and cucumber slaw on a chapati crisp. Top the vegetables with 1 tablespoon of the tuna. Repeat this process with the remaining ingredients. Serve the canapés chilled.

Tuna Nori Rolls with Carrot, Radish, Avocado and Tobiko

Makes 30 Rolls

3 cups sticky rice	4 1/2 cups water
1/4 cup rice wine vinegar	1 tablespoon granulated sugar
6 Nori sheets	2 avocados, peeled and thinly sliced
2 carrots peeled and thinly sliced	1 small daikon radish peeled and thinly sliced
3 scallions, green parts only, sliced lengthwise	2 ounces Tobiko (flying fish roe)
1 pound sushi grade Ahi Tuna sliced into strips	

1. Rinse the rice under cold water, until the water runs clear. Strain the rice well. Place the rice and water in a pot over a medium-high heat. When the water boils, reduce the heat to low and cover the pot. Allow the rice to steam for 20 minutes, or until all of the water has evaporated.

2. Transfer the rice to a bowl. Place the rice wine vinegar, salt and sugar in a small pot over a high heat. When the salt and sugar have dissolved, stir the vinegar into the rice. Using a paddle or wooden spoon, toss the rice to cool it evenly.

3. Lay a Nori sheet on a sushi mat, with a wider edge towards you and the lines on the mat lying horizontal. Leaving 1/2-inch of a wider edge bare, place 1/4 cup of lukewarm rice on the Nori sheet. Press down on the rice, forming a layer between the vegetables and the Nori sheet. In the middle of the rice, place even strips of avocado, carrots, scallions, tuna and daikon. The strips should be parallel to the bare edge of Nori. Sprinkle tobiko over the vegetables and fish. Lightly brush water on the bare edge of the Nori. Using the sushi mat, roll the Nori around the ingredients into a tight cylinder and seal it with the moistened end. Repeat with the remaining ingredients. Cut each roll into 5 pieces. Serve the rolls chilled with soy sauce, wasabi and pickled ginger.

Green Peppercorn Crusted Tuna with Wasabi Aioli on Carrot Crackers

Makes 30 Canapés

Carrot Crackers

1 large carrot
2 cups all-purpose flour
1 teaspoon baking soda
1 egg, slightly beaten
3 tablespoons lard or vegetable shortening, cut into small pieces
1/2 cup water
a pinch of salt
1/4 cup buttermilk

1. Peel and coarsely chop the carrot. Place the carrot and water in a small pot over a medium-high heat. Cover the pot and cook the carrots until they are soft, about 15 minutes. In a blender or food processor, purée the carrots and any juice. Strain the carrot and reserve the juice.

2. In a food processor, combine the flour, salt and baking soda. Add the lard to the flour mixture and pulse until the mixture resembles a coarse meal. Transfer the flour mixture to a mixing bowl. Add the buttermilk, egg and 2 tablespoons of the strained carrot juice to the flour mixture. Mix the ingredients until a firm dough forms. Cover the dough and allow it to rest for 30 minutes in the refrigerator.

3. Preheat the oven to 400°F. On a lightly floured surface, roll the dough 1/8th-inch thick. With a cookie-cutter, cut shapes out of the dough or cut it into squares. Place the shapes on a well-greased baking sheet. Bake the shapes for 5-7 minutes, or until they are slightly brown. Cool the crackers on a grill.

Wasabi Aioli

1 large egg yolk
2 teaspoons rice wine vinegar
1 teaspoon salt
1/4 cup canola oil
1 teaspoon dijon mustard
1 tablespoon wasabi powder
1/2 teaspoon white pepper
1/4 cup olive oil

In a blender or food processor, place the egg yolk, mustard, vinegar, wasabi, salt and pepper. Blend the ingredients until they are frothy. With the machine running, gradually add the oils. Pour the aioli into a squeeze bottle and chill it.

Green Peppercorn Crusted Tuna

1 shallot, finely chopped
1 tablespoon lime juice
4 tablespoons sesame oil
3 tablespoons green peppercorns
salt and pepper
1 teaspoon fresh ginger, peeled and finely chopped

1 garlic clove, finely chopped
1 tablespoon rice wine vinegar
3 tablespoons extra virgin olive oil
1 pound Ahi tuna
1 1/2 cups red-leaf lettuce

1. Whisk together the shallots, garlic, ginger, lime juice, vinegar, 2 tablespoons of the sesame oil and the extra virgin olive oil. Place this ginger vinaigrette aside for 30 minutes.

2. With a spice grinder, coarsely grind the green peppercorns. Place the peppercorns in a small dish. Slice the tuna into 4 rectangular pieces and lightly salt and pepper them. Coat all sides of the tuna pieces with the peppercorns.

3. Place a pan over a high heat. When the pan is hot, add the remaining sesame oil. As soon as the oil is hot, add the tuna pieces. Sear each side of tuna for 2 minutes (for rare). Thinly slice each piece of tuna across the grain of flesh. You should have 30 slices of tuna.

4. Wash the lettuce leaves and tear them into small pieces. Dress the lettuce with the ginger vinaigrette. Place a lettuce leaf on a carrot cracker. Top the lettuce with a slice of tuna. Top the tuna with a squirt of wasabi aioli. Repeat this process with the remaining pieces of tuna. Serve the canapés warm or chilled.

Mahi Mahi with Mango Salsa and Caper Aioli on Crusty Buttermilk Toasts

Makes 40 Canapés

Crusty Buttermilk Toasts

1 tablespoon dry active yeast
1/4 cup warm water, 105-115°F
1/4 cup buttermilk
2 cups all-purpose flour
1 egg white, slightly beaten

1 teaspoon granulated sugar
1 tablespoon vegetable oil
1 teaspoon salt
Cornmeal

1. Sprinkle the yeast and sugar over the warm water. Allow the yeast to rise in a warm, draft-free area until it is foamy, about 10 minutes.

2. Add the oil and buttermilk to the yeast. In a separate bowl, combine the salt and flour. Add the flour to the yeast. Mix the ingredients until a firm dough forms. On a floured surface, knead the dough until it is smooth and elastic, about 10 minutes. Place the dough in an oiled bowl and flip it to oil all sides. Cover the dough and allow it to rise in a warm area until it has doubled in bulk.

3. Preheat the broiler on your oven. Generously sprinkle cornmeal on a baking sheet. Gently deflate the dough and halve it. Stretch each half into a rectangle. Beginning with one of the longer sides, roll the dough into a loaf. Repeat with the other rectangle and place them, seam-sides down on the baking sheet. Slash the top of the loaves twice in a diagonal fashion. Brush the loaves with the egg white and place them under the broiler. After 5 minutes, turn off the broiler and set the oven at 375°F. Allow the loaf to bake for 20 minutes. Cool the loaf completely.

4. Preheat the broiler. Thinly slice the loaf. Lightly toast the slices under the broiler until they are crisp.

Mango Salsa

2 ripe mangoes, peeled
2 tablespoons flat leaf parsley, finely chopped
Juice of 1 lime
2 scallions, finely chopped
1/2 red onion, finely chopped
3 tablespoons fresh cilantro leaves, finely chopped

Cut the flesh of the mangoes off of their seeds. Finely chop the mango flesh and place it in a mixing bowl. Add the scallions, parsley, cilantro and red onion and lime juice. Mix the ingredients well. Refrigerate the salsa.

Caper Aioli

2 large egg yolks
2 teaspoons rice wine vinegar
1/2 teaspoon white pepper
1/4 cup olive oil
3 tablespoons capers
1 tablespoon Dijon mustard
1 teaspoon salt
1/4 cup canola oil
1 tablespoon lemon juice

In a blender or food processor, place the egg yolk, mustard, vinegar, salt and pepper. Blend the ingredients until they are foamy. With the machine running, gradually add the oils. Stir in the lemon juice and capers. Refrigerate the aioli.

Mahi Mahi

2 pounds Mahi Mahi filets
Salt and pepper
2 tablespoons olive oil

1. Slice the Mahi Mahi into bite size pieces. Lightly salt and pepper the pieces. In a shallow pan, heat the oil over a medium-high heat. When the oil is hot add the Mahi Mahi pieces to the pan. Cook the pieces of Mahi Mahi for 3 minutes on each side or until they are cooked through. Depending on the size of your pan, you may need to work in batches.

2. Place 1 tablespoon of mango salsa on a buttermilk toast. Top the salsa with a piece of Mahi Mahi. Top the Mahi Mahi with a squirt of caper aioli. Serve the canapés while the fish is still warm.

Pita Wraps of Sesame Mahi Mahi with Watercress

Makes 40 Canapés

Pita

1 teaspoon dry active yeast
1/2 cup warm water, 105-115°F
1 1/2 cups bread flour

1 tablespoon olive oil
1 tablespoon honey
2 teaspoons salt

1. In a small bowl, combine the yeast, olive oil, warm water and honey. Place the bowl in a warm place for 10 minutes or until it is foamy. In a separate bowl, combine the flour and salt. Gradually add the flour and salt to the yeast mixture. With a wooden spoon, mix the ingredients until a firm dough forms. On a floured surface, knead the dough until it is smooth and elastic, about 10 minutes. Place the dough in an oiled bowl and flip it to oil all sides. Cover the bowl with a towel and place it in a warm place. Let the dough rise until it has doubled in bulk, 1 1/2 to 2 hours.

2. Preheat the oven to 500°F. Gently deflate the dough and divide it into 5 portions. Working with one's palm, flatten each portion of dough into a 1/2-inch thick round. Place the rounds on a floured baking sheet. Allow the rounds to rest for 10 minutes. Heat a baking sheet in the oven. Place the rounds on the baking sheet and bake them until they puff up and brown, about 3 minutes on each side. When cool, peel the layers of each pita apart, forming 10 pitas.

Watercress

1 bunch watercress
1/4 cup raspberries
2 tablespoons granulated sugar
1/2 teaspoon black pepper

2 tablespoons red wine vinegar
2 tablespoons fresh basil leaves
1 teaspoon salt
1/4 cup vegetable oil

Wash the watercress and remove the stems. In a blender combine the vinegar, raspberries, basil, sugar, salt, pepper and oil. Blend the mixture until it is smooth. Toss the watercress in the raspberry dressing.

Sesame Mahi Mahi

1/4 cup sesame seeds
1 1/2 pounds Mahi Mahi filet
salt and pepper
2 tablespoons olive oil

1. Place a pan over a high heat. When the pan is hot add the sesame seeds and toast them until they are brown. Cool the seeds.

2. Slice the Mahi Mahi into 1-inch thick strips. Generously sprinkle sesame seeds over the strips.

3. In a shallow pan, heat half of the olive oil over a medium-high heat. When the oil is hot, add half of the Mahi Mahi strips. Sear the strips for about 3 minutes on each side or until they are cooked through. Transfer the fish to paper towels to remove any excess grease.

4. Working on one edge, place a bed of watercress salad on a pita half. Top the salad with a piece of Mahi Mahi. Roll the pita with the salad and Mahi Mahi inside. Secure the roll by placing toothpicks every inch. Slice the roll between the toothpicks. Repeat this process with the remaining pieces of Mahi Mahi. Serve the canapés warm or chilled.

Fish Cakes with Tropical Dipping Sauce

Makes 50 Canapés

Fish Cakes

- 1 tablespoon olive oil
- 2 jalapeños, seeds and membranes removed and finely chopped
- 1 tablespoon fresh ginger, peeled and chopped
- 3/4 pound medium-sized shrimp, peeled, deveined and coarsely chopped
- 1/4 cup fresh cilantro leaves, chopped
- 1 pound sole filets or other white fish such as cod or halibut
- 1 cup heavy cream, very cold
- 1 tablespoon white pepper
- 3 eggs, thoroughly beaten
- 2 cups canola oil
- 2 shallots, finely chopped
- 2 carrots, peeled and grated
- 3 garlic cloves, finely chopped
- 1/4 cup dry white wine
- 1/4 cup green onions, finely chopped
- 2 egg whites
- 1 tablespoon salt
- 2 cups all-purpose flour
- 3 cups breadcrumbs

1. Heat a pan over a medium-high heat. When the pan is hot add the olive oil. When the oil is hot, add the shallot. Sauté the shallots for 1 minute. Add the Jalapeños to the shallots. Sauté the vegetables for 5 minutes. Add the carrots, ginger and garlic to the shallots. Sauté the vegetables for 5 minutes and add the shrimp. Add the white wine and reduce the wine completely. Continue to cook the shrimp until they are just cooked through. A little under done is good because these shrimp will undergo a second cooking. Transfer the vegetables and shrimp to a bowl and add the cilantro and green onions. Cool the mixture completely.

2. Place the food processor bowl into the freezer 30 minutes prior to use. Coarsely chop the sole filets and purée them in the food processor. With the machine running, add the egg whites. When the sole and egg whites are completely combined, gradually add the cream, salt and pepper. The mousse should be thick and not watery. Chill the mousse.

3. When the shrimp and vegetables are completely cool, fold them into the sole mousse. Form 2 tablespoons of the mousse batter into a small ball. Dredge the ball with flour. Cover the dredged ball with the beaten egg. After wiping off any excess egg, cover the ball with the breadcrumbs. Flatten the ball with the heal of the hand and form it into a cake. Repeat this process with the remaining batter. In a deep pan, heat the canola oil to 325°F. Fry the cakes for 3-4 minutes on each side or until they are golden brown. Dry the cakes on paper towels.

Tropical Dipping Sauce

1 cucumber
1/4 cup fresh mint leaves
1/2 cantaloupe, rind and seeds removed and chopped
1 papaya, peeled, seeded and chopped
Juice of 1/2 lime
1/2 cup sour cream

Peel, deseed and coarsely chop the cucumber. In a blender, purée the cucumber, mint, papaya, cantaloupe and lime juice. Whisk in the sour cream. Serve the sauce chilled with the warm fish cakes.

Poppy Seed Dusted Sea Bass with Radish Slaw on Wonton Chips

Makes 25 Canapés

Wonton Chips

4 cups canola oil
Salt

25 wonton wrappers

Place the oil in a pot over a medium-high heat. When the oil is 375°F, add a few of the wonton wrappers. Fry each wonton for 20 seconds on each side or until they are golden brown. Transfer the chips to paper towels to remove any excess grease. Repeat this process with the remaining wonton wrappers. Lightly dust the chips with salt.

Radish Slaw

1 small daikon radish, peeled
Juice of 1 lime
1 teaspoon ground ginger

2 carrots, peeled
1 tablespoon rice wine vinegar
2 tablespoons olive oil

Using a mandoline or a sharp knife, slice the daikon and carrots into thin strips. In a separate bowl, whisk together the lime juice, vinegar, ginger and olive oil. Toss the daikon and carrot strips in the dressing.

Poppy Seed Dusted Sea Bass

1 pound Sea Bass filet
3 tablespoons poppy seeds

Salt and pepper
2 tablespoons olive oil

1. Slice the Sea Bass into bite-size pieces. Lightly salt and pepper the pieces. Generously sprinkle the Sea Bass with poppy seeds. In a pan, heat the olive oil over a medium-high heat. When the oil is hot, add the pieces of Sea Bass and brown them for 3 minutes on each side or until they are cooked through. Cooking time will vary according to thickness.

2. Place a bed of radish slaw on a wonton chip. Top the slaw with a piece of Sea Bass. Serve the Sea Bass either warm or cold. Do not assemble too many of these ahead of time as the slaw tends to make the wonton chips soggy.

Shellfish

On St. Barth's, I met a Chef that would not stop boasting about her stuffed crab appetizer. When I ordered it, I realized that her proclamations were sincere. She shared with me her secret.

She employs a native woman who has 7 children. On moonlit nights, the children run along the beach and catch any crabs they can get their hands on. The crabs are placed in a wash tub. For the next three days the crabs are fed a strict diet of pineapple, bananas and christophine.

The chef then steams the crabs and picks their meat. The meat is tossed with some citrus, butter and breadcrumbs and placed back in the shell for cooking. The shell is baked until the meat is warm and then brought to your table. The result is a sweet and slightly tangy delight.

Oysters Baked on the Half Shell with Tarragon and Bacon Cream Sauce

Makes 20 Oysters

4 slices of lean bacon, finely chopped
1/4 cup dry white wine
1 teaspoon black pepper, freshly ground
1/4 cup chicken stock or water
1/4 cup heavy cream
1/4 cup Parmesan cheese, grated
2 tablespoons flat leaf parsley leaves, finely chopped
2 green onions, finely chopped
3 tablespoons tarragon leaves, finely chopped
20 fresh oysters, scrubbed

1. In a deep pan over a medium-high heat, place the bacon. Sauté the bacon until it is crisp, about 10 minutes. With a slotted spoon transfer the bacon to paper towels. Strain the grease off of the pan and add the white wine. Increase the heat to high and bring the wine to a boil. Add the chicken broth and reduce the liquid by half. Add the cream and simmer the sauce until it coats a spoon, about 5 minutes. Remove the sauce from the heat and whisk in the Parmesan cheese, parsley, green onions, tarragon and reserved bacon. Keep the sauce warm.

2. Preheat the broiler. Shuck the oysters and place one tablespoon of sauce on each oyster. Place the oysters under the broiler for 5 minutes or until the sauce has browned. Serve the oysters warm.

Oysters Served on the Half Shell with Roasted Beet Vinaigrette

Makes 25 Canapés

3 medium sized beets
2 tablespoons raspberry vinegar
1 tablespoon red wine vinegar
1 shallot, finely chopped
1 garlic clove, finely chopped
1 tablespoon granulated sugar
1/2 cup extra virgin olive oil
20 fresh oysters, scrubbed

1. Preheat the oven to 400°F. Remove the greens from the beets. Delicately scrub the beets under cold water until they are free of dirt. Dry the beets and place them in a roasting pan. Roast the beets for 45 minutes to 1 hour or until their skins swell.

2. Let the beets stand until they are cool enough to handle. Under cold, running water remove the skins from the beets.

3. Coarsely chop the beets. In a blender or food processor, place the beets, raspberry vinegar, red wine vinegar, chopped shallot, garlic, ginger and sugar. Purée the ingredients until they are smooth. With the machine running, slowly add the olive oil. Strain the vinaigrette.

4. Shuck the oysters. Pour 1 tablespoon of vinaigrette on each oyster. Serve the oysters chilled.

Oyster, Bacon and Carrot Brochettes with Caper Tartar

Makes 20 Brochettes

Caper Tartar

1 1/2 cups mayonnaise
3 tablespoons capers
1 tablespoon prepared mustard
1 boiled egg, peeled and finely chopped

1 shallot, minced
2 tablespoons sweet relish
1 tablespoon lemon juice

Whisk together all of the ingredients. Cover and chill the tartar.

Brochettes

20 skewers, soaked overnight
1/2 teaspoon baking soda
1/2 teaspoon ground cumin seed
1/4 teaspoon cayenne pepper
1 cup ice water
10 slices center cut bacon, thinly sliced
4 cups canola oil

1 1/4 cups all-purpose flour
1/2 teaspoon ground turmeric
1/2 teaspoon dark chili powder
1 egg yolk
3 carrots
20 fresh oysters, shucked

1. Sift 1 cup of the flour with the baking soda, turmeric, cumin, chili powder and cayenne pepper. Whisk the egg yolk and ice water into the flour mixture. Allow the batter to rest for 30 minutes in the refrigerator.

2. Wash and peel the carrots. With a mandoline or a sharp knife, slice the carrots into wide, paper thin strips. Plunge the strips into boiling, salted water for 1 minute. Strain the carrots and run cold water over them until they have cooled completely. Dry the carrots on paper towels.

3. Cut the bacon slices in half, forming 20 bacon strips. Place the bacon in a pot and cover it with cold water. Place the pot over a high heat. Bring the bacon to a boil. While removing the foam that forms on the water's surface, simmer the bacon for 15 minutes. Strain the bacon and cool it with cold running water. Dry the bacon on paper towels.

4. Set a bacon slice on a flat surface. Top the bacon with 2 strips of carrot. Place an oyster on one end of the bacon. Roll the bacon and carrots around the oyster and secure it with a skewer. Repeat this process with the remaining oysters.

5. Place the oil in a deep pot over a medium-high heat. When the oil reaches 350°F, dredge the oyster brochettes in the remaining flour. Dip a brochette into the batter and then into the hot oil. Fry the brochette for 2 minutes or until it is golden brown. Repeat this process with the remaining brochettes. Remove any excess grease by patting the brochettes with paper towels. Serve the brochettes while they are still warm with the caper tartar in a bowl for dipping.

Pickled Clams with Tomato and Oregano Relish on Wonton Chips

Makes 20 Canapés

Pickled Clams

1 tablespoon olive oil
2 pounds of Quahog Clams,
   with shells scrubbed and rinsed
3 tablespoons soy sauce
3 tablespoons granulated sugar
2 scallions, green parts only, chopped

1 shallot, finely chopped

1/2 cup dry white wine
2 tablespoons rice wine vinegar
2 tablespoons lemon juice
1/4 teaspoon ground cardamom

1. Place the olive oil in a deep pot over a medium-high heat. When the oil is hot, add the shallots. Sauté the shallots for 1 minute. Add the clams and increase the heat to high. Add the wine and cover the pot. Steam the clams for 10 minutes, or until most of them have opened. Remove the clams from the pot and strain the cooking liquid. Discard any clams that did not open.

2. Remove the clams from their shells and place them in a bowl. In a separate bowl, whisk together the cooking liquid and the remaining ingredients. Pour the marinade over the clams and refrigerate them for at least 8 hours.

Tomato and Oregano Relish

3 tomatoes
2 garlic cloves, chopped
3 oregano sprigs
1/4 cup fresh oregano leaves, chopped

1 shallot, finely chopped
2 thyme sprigs
1 tablespoon olive oil

1. Preheat oven to 250°F. Core the tomatoes. With a paring knife mark the bottom of each tomato with an X. Plunge the tomatoes in a pot of boiling water for 1 minute or until their skins begin to come off. Transfer the tomatoes to a bowl of ice water. Once they have cooled, peel the skins off of the tomatoes. Cut the tomatoes into quarters. Remove the membranes and seeds from the quarters, forming tomato petals. Place the tomato petals, shallots, garlic, thyme and oregano stems in a roasting pan. Drizzle the olive oil over the tomatoes. Place the roasting pan in the oven and allow the tomatoes to roast for 1 hour.

2. Discard the thyme and oregano sprigs. Place the tomato petals on a grill to drain for 20 minutes. Coarsely chop the tomatoes and add the oregano leaves. Chill the relish.

Wonton Chips

2 cups corn oil
10 wonton wrappers

1. Place the oil in a stainless steel pot over a medium-high heat. Cut the wonton wrappers in half to form triangles. When the oil reaches 375°F add a few wonton triangles. Fry each triangle for 30 seconds on each side or until they are golden brown. Transfer the triangles to paper towels to remove any excess grease. Repeat this process with the remaining wonton wrappers.

2. Place one tablespoon of tomato and oregano relish on a wonton chip. Top the relish with a pickled clam. Serve immediately. The relish will make the chips soggy so assemble only as much as you need.

Fresh Herb Clam Stuffing on Bagel Chips with Roasted Red Peppers

Makes 45 Canapés

Bagel Chips

1/4 cup milk
1 tablespoon dry active yeast
2 3/4 cups bread flour
1 tablespoon unsalted butter, melted
Olive oil

1/4 cup water
1 teaspoon granulated sugar
1/2 tablespoon salt
1 egg, separated

1. In a small pot over a high heat, combine the milk and water. Heat the milk and water to 105-115°F. Sprinkle the yeast and the sugar over the warm liquid. Place the yeast mixture in a warm place for 10 minutes, or until it is foamy.

2. In a bowl, combine the flour and salt and form them into a fountain. Place the yeast, butter and remaining water and milk in the center of the fountain. Lightly beat the egg white and add it to the center. Gradually combine the wet and dry ingredients to form a soft dough. Knead the dough for 15 minutes or until it is smooth and elastic. Place the dough in an oiled bowl. Flip the dough to oil all sides. Cover the dough with plastic wrap and let it rise in a warm place until it has doubled in bulk.

3. On a floured surface, gently deflate the dough and divide it into 10 pieces. Roll each portion into a 2-inch long rope. After brushing the ends with water, press them together to form small bagels.

4. Preheat the oven to 425°F. In a pot of simmering water, place the bagels. Poach each bagel for 90 seconds on each side or until they have puffed up. Shaking off any excess moisture, place the bagels on a parchment paper lined baking sheet. Brush the bagels with the egg yolk and bake them for 5-10 minutes or until they are golden brown. Cool the bagels on a grill.

5. Preheat the oven to 400°F. Forming rounds, thinly slice each bagel,. Brush the slices with olive oil and bake them until they are crisp, about 5 minutes.

Roasted Red Peppers

2 red peppers

1. Preheat the broiler. Wash the peppers. Place the peppers close to the broiler. Turn the peppers as their skins blister. When the peppers are completely blistered, transfer them to a bowl. Tightly cover the bowl with plastic wrap and place it in the refrigerator.

2. When the peppers are completely cool, remove their skins, seeds and membranes. Finely dice the peppers.

Clam Stuffing

2 tablespoons olive oil	2 shallots, finely chopped
2 garlic cloves, peeled and smashed	4 pounds littleneck clams, scrubbed and picked over
1/2 cup red wine	1/2 cup oyster mushrooms, thinly sliced
1 tablespoon fresh ginger, peeled and finely chopped	1/2 cup breadcrumbs
1/4 cup Parmesan cheese, grated	2 tablespoons mozzarella, grated
2 tablespoons fresh oregano leaves, finely chopped	3 green onions, finely chopped
1 tablespoon fresh mint leaves, finely chopped	1/4 cup flat leaf parsley leaves, finely chopped
1/4 cup sweet butter, melted	

1. Place 1 tablespoon of the olive oil in a pan over a medium-high heat. When the oil is hot, add the shallots and sauté them for 1 minute. Increase the heat to high. Add the garlic and the clams to the pot and heat them for 30 seconds. Add the red wine and cover the pot tightly. Steam the clams for 10 minutes or until they have all opened. Discard any clams that fail to open. Strain the cooking liquid and set it aside. Remove the clams from their shells and set a few shells aside for decoration. Coarsely chop half of the clams.

2. Place the remaining olive oil in a shallow pan over medium-high heat. When the oil is hot, add the oyster mushrooms and the ginger to the pan. Sauté the oyster mushrooms until they are limp, about 5 minutes.

3. Preheat the oven to 400°F. In a bowl, combine the cooking liquid, chopped clams, mushrooms, breadcrumbs, Parmesan, mozzarella, oregano, green onions, mint, parsley, and melted butter. Place the mixture in a casserole dish and bake it for 20 minutes or until the cheese has melted.

4. Place 1 tablespoon of fresh herb clam stuffing on a bagel chip. Top the stuffing with 1 teaspoon of the roasted red peppers and a whole clam. Decorate the canapés with fresh herbs. Serve the canapés warm.

Clam and Corn Fritters with Blue Cheese and Basil Dressing

Makes 30 Canapés

Blue Cheese and Basil Dressing

1 tablespoon lemon juice
1 cup mayonnaise
1 tablespoon milk

1/4 cup crumbled blue cheese
2 tablespoons chopped fresh basil leaves
1 teaspoon black pepper

Whisk together all of the ingredients and chill the dressing.

Clam and Corn Fritters

2 eggs, separated

1/4 cup all purpose flour
1/2 teaspoon black pepper
1 cup corn kernels
1/4 cup canola oil

2 tablespoons flat leaf parsley, finely chopped
1 teaspoon salt
1 1/2 cups ground clams, well drained
1 cup cheddar cheese

Whisk the egg yolks until they are foamy. Gradually whisk in the parsley, flour, salt and pepper. Add the ground clams, corn and cheddar cheese and incorporate the mixture completely. Whisk the egg whites until they hold stiff peaks. Fold the whites into the batter. Heat a skillet over a medium-high flame. Add the canola oil to the skillet and allow it to heat. Working in batches, drop tablespoonfuls of the batter onto the hot skillet and fry them until golden brown, about 5 minutes on each side. Remove the fritters from the skillet and pat them with paper towels to remove excess grease. Serve the dressing along side the warm fritters.

Glazed Shrimp with Oregano Roasted Shallots on French Bread

Makes 45 Canapés

French Bread

1 tablespoon dry active yeast
1 cup warm water, 105-110°F
3 cups all purpose flour

1 teaspoon granulated sugar
1 tablespoon salt
Cornmeal

1. Sprinkle the yeast and sugar over 1/2 cup of the warm water. Allow the yeast to rise in a warm, draft free area until it is foamy, about 10 minutes.

2. In a separate bowl, combine the salt and flour. Add the yeast and the remaining water to the flour. With a wooden spoon, mix the ingredients until a shaggy dough forms.

3. On a floured surface, knead the dough until it is smooth and elastic, about 10 minutes. Place the dough in an oiled bowl and flip it to oil all sides. Cover the dough and allow it to rise in a warm, draft free area until it has doubled in bulk.

4. Preheat the oven to 400°F. Generously sprinkle cornmeal on a baking sheet. Gently deflate the dough and divide it in half. Pull one half into a rectangle. Beginning at a larger end, roll the dough into a loaf. Repeat with the second half. Place the loaves, seam sides down, on the baking sheets. Allow the loaves to double in size in a warm, draft free area. Slash the top of each loaf three times and bake them for 35 minutes.

5. Cool the loaves completely and cut them into 1/2-inch thick slices.

Oregano Roasted Shallots

5 large shallots
1 tablespoon olive oil
3 tablespoons fresh oregano leaves, finely chopped

1. Preheat the oven to 400°F. Toss the shallots in the olive oil and place them in a roasting pan. Place the shallots in the oven for 20 minutes or until their skins swell.

2. Cool the shallots completely. Remove the roots and skins from the shallots and thinly slice them. Add the oregano to the shallots and toss to combine.

Glazed Shrimp

1/4 cup Worcestershire sauce
3 garlic cloves, finely chopped
juice of 2 lemons
2 tablespoons water
1 tablespoon half-cracked black pepper
2 pounds large Shrimp, peeled and deveined
2 tablespoons cold unsalted butter, cut into pieces
1/4 cup fresh parsley, chopped

1. In a shallow pan, whisk together the Worcestershire sauce, garlic, pepper and lemon juice. Place the pan over a high heat. Add the shrimp and toss them in the sauce. Reduce the heat to medium-high and simmer until the shrimp are almost cooked through. Gradually add the butter to the pan and whisk the sauce until the butter has emulsified into the sauce. If your sauce breaks just bring it to a boil and it will re-emulsify.

2. Place a few shallot slices on a piece of French bread. Top the shallots with 1 or 2 shrimps. Repeat this process with the remaining shrimp and serve while the shrimp are still warm.

Rock Shrimp Wontons with Spicy Honey

Makes 30 Canapés

Spicy Honey

2 cups honey
1/4 cup orange juice
2 fresh jalapeños, finely chopped

2 tablespoons red pepper flakes
2 tablespoons lime juice

Whisk together all of the ingredients and let sit for at least 30 minutes. The longer this sauce sits the more flavorful it will be.

Rock Shrimp Wontons

1 pound rock shrimp, rinsed (another type of shrimp may be substituted)
1/4 cup fresh mint leaves, finely chopped
1/4 cup fresh parsley leaves, finely chopped
2 small shallots, finely chopped
30 wonton wrappers
2 eggs beaten with 2 tablespoons water
4 cups canola oil

1. Place the bowl and blade for the food processor into the freezer for 15 minutes. Pick over the rock shrimp for any loose bits of shell. In the food processor, purée the first 4 ingredients until they are smooth. Working on a flat surface, lay out one of the wonton wrappers. Place a tablespoon of the shrimp mixture into the center of the wrapper. Brush the edges of the wrapper with the egg wash. Bring two of the corners up to meet each other, forming a triangle. Making sure to get all of the air out of the stuffing, seal the sides of the triangle by pressing them together. Repeat this process with the remaining wontons.

2. In a pot, heat the oil to 350ºF. Working in batches, fry the wontons for 5 minutes, or until they are cooked through. Transfer the wontons to paper towels to remove any excess grease. Serve the wontons while they are still hot with the spicy honey on the side.

Boiled Crawfish with Cantaloupe Papaya Salad on Sesame Crackers

Makes 30 Canapés

Sesame Crackers

1 cup all purpose flour
1/4 teaspoon baking soda
1/8 cup buttermilk
1 1/2 tablespoons lard or vegetable shortening, cold

1/4 teaspoon salt
1 egg, slightly beaten
2 tablespoons white sesame seeds

Preheat the oven to 400°F. In a food processor bowl, combine the flour, salt and baking soda. Cut the lard into small pieces and add them to the dry ingredients. Pulse the ingredients until they form a coarse meal. Transfer the dry ingredients into a large bowl. In a separate bowl, whisk together the egg, buttermilk and sesame seeds. Stir the egg mixture into the flour mixture, until a firm dough forms. On a lightly floured surface, roll out the dough to 1/8th inch thick. Cut shapes out of the dough. Place the shapes on a greased baking sheet. Bake the shapes until they are slightly brown, about 6-8 minutes.

Boiled Crawfish

1/2 yellow onion, chopped
3 parsley stems
1 bay leaf
1 Anaheim chili, cored, seeded and chopped
1 tablespoon paprika
1/4 cup dry white wine
2 pounds whole live crawfish

2 celery stalks, chopped
2 thyme sprigs
5 black peppercorns
2 garlic cloves, chopped
1 teaspoon cayenne pepper
1 gallon cold water
1 quart of ice

Place in a pot the onion, celery, parsley stems, thyme sprigs, bay leaf, peppercorns, chili, garlic, paprika, cayenne, wine and water. Place the pot over a high heat. Bring the liquid to a boil and reduce the heat to a simmer. Lightly simmer the liquid for 10 minutes. Add the washed crawfish to the pot and cook them for 10-15 minutes, depending on their size. Test their doneness, by extracting one crawfish and separating the tail from the body. If the meat is bright red, the crawfish are cooked. Remove the pot from the heat and add the ice. Allow the crawfish to stand for 15 minutes. This last step infuses more flavor into the crawfish without overcooking them. Remove the meat from the crawfish tails and discard the shells or use them in a nice bisque.

Cantaloupe Papaya Salad

1/2 cantaloupe, peeled and seeded
1 papaya, peeled and seeded
Juice of 1 lime

1. Finely chop the cantaloupe and papaya. In a bowl, combine the fruit and add the lime juice.

2. Place 1 tablespoon of cantaloupe papaya salad on a sesame cracker. Top the salad with a crawfish tail. Repeat this process with the remaining crawfish tails. Serve immediately.

Green Crawfish Cakes with Roasted Red Pepper Aioli

Makes 40 Canapés

Red Pepper Aioli

2 red peppers
1 tablespoon Dijon mustard
1 tablespoon rice wine vinegar
1/2 teaspoon white pepper
1/2 cup olive oil

2 egg yolks
1 garlic clove, finely chopped
1/2 teaspoon salt
1/2 cup canola oil

1. Preheat the broiler. Wash the red peppers. Place the peppers close to the broiler. Turn the peppers as their skins blister. When their skins have completely blistered, place the peppers in an airtight container and chill them. When they are cool, remove the skins, seeds and membranes from the peppers and chop them finely.

2. In a food processor, combine the red peppers, egg yolk, mustard, garlic, rice wine vinegar, salt and pepper. Process the mixture until it is frothy. While the machine is running, gradually add the oils. Chill the aioli.

Green Crawfish Cakes

1 pound crawfish tails, chopped
1 poblano chili, cored, seeds and membranes removed
2 shallots, finely chopped
2 garlic cloves, chopped
1 teaspoon salt
16 crushed soda crackers

1/2 pound spinach leaves
1 tablespoon olive oil
3 scallions, chopped
1/4 cup fresh basil leaves, chopped
1 teaspoon pepper

1. Remove the stems from the spinach. Remove any dirt from the spinach by swishing the leaves in a bowl of cold water.

2. Chop the poblano. In a food processor, purée the poblano, spinach, shallots, scallions, garlic, basil, salt and pepper. While the machine is running, gradually add the cracker crumbs. When the ingredients are incorporated, transfer them to a mixing bowl and fold in the crawfish meat. Form the batter into 2 tablespoon sized patties and chill the patties for 30 minutes.

3. Preheat the oven to 350°F. Place the patties on a nonstick baking sheet. Bake the patties for 5 minutes. Flip the patties and bake them for another 3 minutes. Green crawfish cakes are excellent warm or chilled. Serve the aioli in a chilled serving dish on the side.

Crab Tempura with Spicy Tomato Dipping Sauce

Makes 20 Canapés

Spicy Tomato Dipping Sauce

1 stalk fresh lemon grass
1 shallot, finely chopped
1 teaspoon green chili paste
1/4 cup red wine
1 cup + 1 tablespoon water

1 tablespoon olive oil
1 tablespoon fresh ginger, peeled and chopped
2 tomatoes, chopped
1 bay leaf
1 tablespoon cornstarch

1. Lay the lemon grass stalk on a cutting board. Cut off the root and discard it. With the smooth side of a mallet or a small pot, pound the white part of the lemon grass until it breaks apart. Finely chop the white part and discard the tough, green stalk.

2. In a shallow pan over a medium heat, place the olive oil. When the oil is hot, add the shallots, lemon grass, ginger and chili paste. Sauté the ingredients for 1 minute. Add the tomatoes and sauté them for 20 minutes or until they break up in the pan. Increase the heat to high and add the red wine. Simmer the red wine for 3 minutes and then add 1 cup of the water and the bay leaf. Reduce the heat to medium-high and simmer the mixture for 10 minutes to infuse the flavors. The mixture should be watery.

3. Whisk together the cornstarch and the remaining water. Add the cornstarch mixture to the tomatoes. Simmer the tomatoes for an additional 10 minutes, or until the sauce is thick. Remove the bay leaf and liquidize the sauce in a blender. Serve the sauce warm.

Crab Tempura

3 ounces flaked crabmeat
3 eggs
3/4 cup ice water
1/2 teaspoon salt

3 tablespoons cracker crumbs, finely ground
10 ounces lump crabmeat
1 cup all purpose flour
3 cups corn oil

1. With a fork, combine the flaked crabmeat, cracker crumbs and one beaten egg. Divide the 10 ounces of lump crabmeat into 20 lumps. Cover a lump of crabmeat with 1 teaspoon of the cracker crumb mixture. With floured hands form the lump of crabmeat into a small ball. Repeat this process with the remaining lumps. Refrigerate the balls for one hour.

2. Whisk together the remaining egg, ice water, flour and salt. Allow the batter to rest for 30 minutes.

3. In a small pot, heat the corn oil to 350°F. Working in batches, dip the balls into the batter and then fry them in the oil until they are golden brown, about 45 seconds. Transfer the balls to paper towels to remove any excess grease. Serve the Crab Tempura warm with toothpicks and the sauce on the side.

Crabmeat, Capers and Fennel Stuffed in Mushroom Caps

Makes 25 Mushrooms

25 large mushroom caps	1 tablespoon unsalted butter
1 large head of fennel, stalks and core removed	2 tablespoons olive oil
1 shallot, finely chopped	2 carrots, peeled and finely chopped
1/4 cup sweet white wine	1/4 cup capers
1/4 cup grated Parmesan cheese	1 pound lump crabmeat
2 tablespoons flat leaf parsley leaves, chopped	2 tablespoons bread crumbs

1. Wash the mushroom caps. Sprinkle the caps with salt and pepper. In a pan over medium-high heat, melt the butter. When the butter stops foaming add the mushroom caps. Partially cover the mushrooms and cook them for 3 minutes on each side, or until they are cooked through but still firm. Strain the mushrooms.

2. Remove any tough outer leaves from the fennel and finely chop it. In a pan, heat the olive oil over a medium-high heat. When the oil is hot, add the shallot, fennel and carrot. Sauté the vegetables for 10 minutes or until they are tender. Increase the heat to high and add the wine. Reduce the wine completely and remove the vegetables from the heat.

3. In a mixing bowl, combine the vegetables, capers, Parmesan, crabmeat, parsley and bread crumbs. Spoon the stuffing into the mushroom caps. Place the caps under a preheated broiler for 5 minutes. Serve the mushrooms warm.

Crab Salad in Lettuce Pouches

Makes 20 Canapés

3 carrots, peeled
1 tablespoon olive oil
1 garlic clove, finely chopped
10 oz lump crabmeat
1 teaspoon salt
1/4 cup fresh cilantro leaves, chopped

2 shallots
3 celery stalks, finely chopped
1/2 cup dry white wine
1 tablespoon paprika
1 teaspoon white pepper
10 leaves of red leafed lettuce

1. With a mandoline or peeler, slice thin strips of carrot. Plunge the carrot strips into a pot of boiling, salted water. Transfer the strips to a bowl of ice water and cool them completely. Dry the carrot strips on a dish towel.

2. Finely chop the shallots. In a shallow pan over a medium-high heat, place the olive oil. When the oil is hot, add the shallots. Sauté the shallots for 1 minute. Finely chop the celery and add it to the shallots. Sauté the celery until it is tender, about 5 minutes. Add the chopped garlic and white wine and increase the heat to high. Reduce the wine almost completely. Add the crabmeat, paprika, salt, pepper, ginger powder and cilantro to the pan and remove the pan from the heat. Drain and cool the crab salad.

3. Remove the ribs from the lettuce leaves and cut them into squares. Place 1 tablespoon of the crab salad on a lettuce square. Roll the lettuce around the salad, tucking in the ends. Wrap a carrot around the lettuce pouch and secure it with a toothpick. Serve the pouches chilled.

Basil and Pink Grapefruit Scallops with Mixed Greens on Anise Crackers

Makes 30 Canapés

Anise Crackers

2 cups all purpose flour
1 teaspoon baking soda
1 beaten egg
1/4 cup buttermilk

1 teaspoon salt
1/4 cup cold lard, cut into small pieces
1 tablespoon anise seeds

1. Sift the flour, salt and baking soda together. Cut the shortening into the dry ingredients until it resembles a coarse meal. Form these ingredients into a well. In the center of the well add the egg, anise seed and buttermilk. Gradually incorporate the wet and dry ingredients until a firm dough forms.

2. Preheat the oven to 400°F. On a floured surface, roll the dough paper thin and cut it into shapes. Place the shapes on a nonstick baking sheet. Bake the crackers for 7 minutes or until they are brown. Allow the crackers to cool completely, on a grill.

Grapefruit and Basil Scallops

2 pink grapefruits
Salt and pepper
1/4 cup dry white wine
1 1/2 cups mixed greens, washed and dried

1 pound Bay Scallops, tough outer mussels removed
1 tablespoon sweet butter
1/4 cup fresh basil leaves, chopped

1. With a sharp knife, cut the rind off of the grapefruit. Run the knife along the membranes of the grapefruits to remove the sections.

2. Lightly salt and pepper the scallops. In a shallow pan, over a medium heat, melt half the butter. When the butter has stopped foaming, add half of the scallops. Brown the scallops for 1 minute on each side. Transfer the scallops to a plate. Repeat this process with the remaining scallops. Return all of the scallops to the pan and increase the heat to high. Add the wine and grapefruit sections. Cook the scallops for 2 minutes or until they are cooked through. Strain the scallops. Cool the scallops and add the basil.

3. Place a few greens on an anise cracker. Top the greens with 2 scallops. Repeat this process with the remaining scallops. Serve the scallops chilled.

Cardamom Scallops with Celeriac Purée on Brown Bread

Makes 30 Canapés

Brown Bread

1 3/4 cups whole wheat flour
1 cup warm water, 105-115°F
1 tablespoon salt

1 tablespoon dry active yeast
1 tablespoon blackstrap molasses

1. Heat the oven to 200°F. Place the whole wheat flour in a pan and place it in the oven. The flour should be warm when mixing the bread. Sprinkle the yeast over 1/4 cup of the warm water. Add the molasses to the water. Allow the yeast to rise in a draft free area, for 10 minutes or until it is foamy.

2. When the yeast is foamy, add the remaining warm water. In a separate bowl, combine the salt and the warm flour. Add the flour to the yeast mixture. Mix the ingredients until a sticky dough forms. Pour the dough into a well buttered loaf pan and cover it. Allow the dough to rise in a draft free area. Preheat the oven to 450°F. When the dough has risen one-third of its original size, place the pans in the oven to bake for 40 minutes.

3. Allow the bread to cool completely on a grill. Slice the loaves thinly. Cut the slices in half and toast them briefly under the broiler.

Celeriac Purée

1 celeriac head
1 tablespoon salt

4 cups milk
1 teaspoon white pepper

1. Peel the celeriac and cut it into cubes. Place the cubes in a pot and cover them with the milk. Place the pot over a medium heat and allow the celeriac to simmer for 30 minutes, or until the cubes are tender. Strain and cool the celeriac.

2. In a blender or food processor, purée the celeriac until it is smooth. With the machine running, add the salt and pepper. Keep the purée warm.

Cardamom Scallops

2 shallots, finely chopped
1/4 teaspoon ground cardamom
1/4 cup soy sauce
1 teaspoon cornstarch
30 Sea scallops

1 tablespoon olive oil
1 tablespoon fresh ginger, peeled and chopped
1 tablespoon blackstrap molasses
1/4 cup chicken broth or water
1 tablespoon unsalted butter

1. Place the olive oil in a shallow pan over a medium-high heat. When the oil is hot, add the shallot to the pan and sauté it. When the shallot is translucent add the cardamom, ginger, soy sauce and molasses. Whisk together the cornstarch and chicken broth. Add the broth to the sauce. Simmer the sauce for 10 minutes or until it is thick. Strain the sauce and set it aside.

2. Remove the tough muscle from each scallop. In a pan over a medium-high heat, place the butter. When the butter begins to sizzle, add the scallops. Brown the scallops for 1 minute on each side. Increase the heat to high and add the sauce to the pan. Simmer the sauce over a medium-high heat. Remove the scallops from the pan when they are thoroughly glazed, about 5 minutes.

3. Place 1 tablespoon of celeriac purée on a slice of brown bread. Top the celeriac with a scallop. Serve the canapés warm.

Spicy Glazed Scallops

Makes 30 Canapés

1 tablespoon + 1/3 cup sesame oil
1 small yellow onion, chopped
1 leek, white parts only, chopped
1 red pepper, stem, core and seeds removed, chopped
1 carrot, peeled and chopped
2 stalks celery with leaves, chopped
1/4 cup brown sugar
4 dried chili d'arbols
1/2 cup sake
30 large scallops
3 tablespoons olive oil

1. Heat 1 tablespoon of sesame oil, in a pot over a high heat. When the oil shimmers, add the onions and reduce the heat to medium. Slowly cook the onions until they are brown and wilted about 15 minutes. Add the leek, red pepper, carrot and celery and increase the heat to medium-high. Cook the vegetables until they are soft. Stir in the brown sugar and chilis and cook until the brown sugar coats the vegetables, about 3 minutes. Add the sake and reduce by half. Blend the mixture in a blender or food processor. With the machine running, add the remaining sesame oil. Set the sauce aside.

2. Preheat the oven to 400°F. Remove the tough muscle from the scallops. Heat one tablespoon of the olive oil in a pan over a high heat. When the oil is hot, add some the scallops. Sear each scallop on one side for two minutes. Flip the scallops and coat the top of each one with a teaspoon of spicy glaze. Finish cooking the scallops in the oven. The glaze will melt over the scallops. Repeat this process with the remaining scallops. Serve the scallops warm with toothpicks.

Scallop Seviche with Tomato and Avocado Salsa on Whole Wheat Toasts

Makes 40 Canapés

Whole Wheat Toasts

1 teaspoon dry active yeast
1/4 cup warm water, 105-115°F
2 cups whole wheat flour
1/2 cup all-purpose flour
1 tablespoon cornmeal

1/2 teaspoon granulated sugar
1/2 cup warm milk, 105-115°F
1/2 cup finely ground rye flour
1 tablespoon salt

1. Sprinkle the yeast and sugar over the warm water. Allow the yeast rise in a warm, draft free area for 10 minutes or until it is foamy.

2. Add the warm milk to the yeast mixture. In a separate bowl, combine the flours and salt. Gradually add the flours and the salt to the wet ingredients, until a firm dough forms. Knead the dough until it is smooth and elastic, about 15 minutes. Place the dough in an oiled bowl. Flip the dough to oil all sides. Cover the dough and allow it to rise in a warm place, until it has doubled in bulk.

3. Preheat the oven to 350°F. On a floured surface, gently deflate the dough and knead it for 10 minutes. Shape the dough into 2 small loaves. Sprinkle the cornmeal on a baking sheet and place the loaves on it, seam-sides down. Cover the loaves and allow them to rise until they are doubled in bulk. Place the loaves in the oven and bake them for 35 minutes. Cool the loaves completely on a grill.

4. Preheat the broiler. Thinly slice the loaves and toast them under the broiler until they are golden brown.

Scallop Seviche

1/2 cup lemon juice
1/2 cup lime juice
1/4 cup orange juice
1 tablespoon chopped lemon zest
1 tablespoon chopped lime zest
1/4 cup fresh cilantro leaves, chopped
1 small yellow onion, chopped
1 red pepper, cored, seeded and finely chopped
2 jalapeños, cored, seeded and finely chopped
2 garlic cloves, chopped
1 pound small Bay scallops, tough muscles removed

1. Combine the lemon juice, lime juice, orange juice, lemon zest, lime zest, cilantro, onion, red pepper, jalapeños, and garlic. Set the dressing aside for thirty minutes.

2. Place the scallops in a colander and rinse them thoroughly. Place the scallops in the marinade and refrigerate them for 1-2 hours. The scallops should be firm.

Tomato and Avocado Salsa

2 ripe tomatoes
1 ripe avocado
1 teaspoon salt
1 teaspoon black pepper

1. Remove the cores from the tomatoes and cut them into quarters. Remove the seeds from the tomatoes and finely dice them.

2. Halve and peel the avocado. Remove the pit and finely chop the avocado. Combine the avocado, tomato, salt and pepper.

3. Place a spoonful of salsa on a whole wheat toast. Top the salsa with a few of the scallops. Spoon 1 teaspoon of the marinade over the scallops. Repeat this process with the remaining scallops. Serve the canapés chilled.

Miso Lobster with Endive Chiffonade in Choux Pastry

Makes 25 Canapés

Choux Pastry

1/3 cup unsalted butter
1 cup all purpose flour
1 teaspoon granulated sugar
1 cup water
1 teaspoon salt
4 eggs

1. In a deep pot, bring the butter and water to a boil. Add the flour, salt and sugar into the boiling water. With a wooden spoon, stir this dough vigorously over a medium-high heat. When the dough forms into a ball, remove it from the heat. Adding one egg at a time, mix the eggs into the choux dough. Transfer the choux dough to a pastry bag.

2. Preheat the oven to 400°F. Leaving plenty of space between each pastry, pipe the choux dough into 2-inch long shells, on to a parchment paper lined baking sheet. Place the choux pastries into the oven. Steam helps choux pastry rise, so do not open the oven for at least 10 minutes. Bake the choux pastry for 20-25 minutes or until they are golden brown. Remove the pastries from the oven and allow them to cool completely, on a grill. With a sharp knife, cut off the tops of each pastry and hollow out the middle.

Lobster In Miso Sauce

2 medium-sized shell-on lobster tails, each halved lengthwise
2 tablespoons sesame oil
2 garlic cloves, chopped
1 tablespoon fresh ginger, peeled chopped
1 tablespoon soy sauce
3/4 cup chicken broth or water
2 tablespoons miso
1 teaspoon granulated sugar
1/2 cup sherry
1 teaspoon cornstarch

1. Place a skillet or wok over a medium-high heat. When the skillet is hot, add the lobster tails, sesame oil, miso and garlic. When the lobster tails are covered with miso, add the sugar, ginger and sherry and reduce the sherry by half. Add the soy sauce and continue to simmer the liquid. With a slotted spoon transfer the lobster tails to a plate. Cover the lobster tails and keep them in a warm place. Whisk the cornstarch into the broth. Continue to simmer the sauce until it covers the back of the spoon.

2. Pick the meat out of the shells and keep it in a warm place.

Endive Chiffonade

2 heads of endive
1 lemon, halved

1. Halve the endive heads and remove the cores. To prevent discoloration, rub the endive with the cut side of the lemon. Crosscut the endive heads.

2. Toss the lobster in the warm sauce. Fill a spoonful of endive into a choux pasty and top with two pieces of lobster meat. Serve while the lobster meat is still warm.

Steamed Mussels with Cucumber Cardamom Sauce

Makes 30 Canapés

2 ripe tomatoes
1 bay leaf
2 tablespoons flat leaf parsley leaves, finely chopped
2 pounds fresh mussels
1 shallot, finely chopped
1 cucumber, peeled, seeded and finely chopped
1/4 cup heavy cream

2 garlic cloves, finely chopped
3 thyme sprigs
2 tablespoons fresh mint leaves, chopped
1 tablespoon olive oil
1 cup dry white wine
1 teaspoon ground cardamom

1. Core the tomatoes. With a paring knife, mark the bottoms of the tomatoes with X's. Plunge the tomatoes in a pot of boiling water for 1 minute or until the skins begin to come off. Transfer the tomatoes to a bowl of ice water. Remove the skins from the tomatoes. Cut the tomatoes in half and remove the seeds by squeezing a tomato half. Coarsely chop the tomatoes.

2. Place the tomatoes, garlic, bay leaf and thyme in a shallow pan. Cover the pan and place it over a medium-low heat for 15 minutes or until the tomatoes break up. Take the tomatoes off of the heat and remove the bay leaf and thyme sprigs. Add the chopped parsley and mint to the tomatoes.

3. Wash the mussels and remove any beards. Discard any broken mussels or any that don't shut when rapped against a hard service. Place the olive oil in a deep pot, over a medium-high heat. When the oil is hot, add the shallots and sauté them for 1 minute. When the shallots are tender, add the mussels and increase the heat to high. Heat the mussels for 15 seconds. Add the white wine and cover the pot tightly. Steam the mussels for 10 minutes, or until most of them have opened. Remove the mussels from the liquid. Discard any unopened mussels.

4. Simmer the cooking liquid over a medium-high heat for 2 minutes. Strain the cooking liquid into a sauce pan and add the tomatoes, cardamom, and heavy cream. Simmer the sauce for an additional 5 minutes or until the sauce coats a spoon. Add the cucumber and remove the sauce from the heat.

5. Discard the top shell of each mussel. Cover the mussel on the half shell with some of the sauce. Serve the mussels warm or chilled.

Poultry

I spent one Thanksgiving in the South Pacific. Craving roasted turkey, my travel partner and I were determined to find a proper Thanksgiving dinner. Most of the restaurants we phoned regretfully admitted there was little demand for a Thanksgiving dinner with all of the trimmings.

I watched as my travel partner phoned the final number. She asked, " Are you serving turkey dinner this evening?" She paused and a large smile broke out on her face. My mouth watering, I asked, "What did they say?" Suppressing a giggle, my travel mate looked at me and said, "They asked me, 'What's turkey?'"

Julienne of Chicken Breast with Braised Caper and Tomato Sauce on Fresh Herb Focaccia

Makes 30 Canapés

Fresh Herb Focaccia

1 teaspoon dry active yeast
1/2 cup warm water, 105-115°F
1 3/4 cups bread flour
1/4 cup fresh basil leaves, finely chopped
Coarse sea salt

1/4 teaspoon granulated sugar
1 tablespoon olive oil
1 teaspoon salt
1/4 cup fresh oregano leaves, finely chopped

1. Sprinkle the yeast and sugar over 1/4 cup of the warm water. Allow the yeast to rise in a warm, draft free area for 10 minutes, or until it is foamy.

2. Add the remaining water and olive oil to the yeast. In a separate bowl, combine the flour and salt. Gradually add the flour to the yeast, until a firm dough forms. On a floured surface, knead the dough for 10 minutes. The dough should be smooth and elastic. Place the dough in an oiled bowl and flip it to oil all sides. Cover the dough and allow it to rise in a warm area until it has doubled in bulk.

3. Preheat the oven to 425°F. Gently deflate the dough and knead in the basil and oregano leaves. Pat the dough flat on a floured baking sheet. Cover the dough and allow it to rise until it has doubled in bulk.

4. Forming a grid of dents, press into the top of the dough with one's fingers. Sprinkle the dough with coarse salt and bake it for 30-35 minutes. Cool the focaccia completely on a grill. Slice the focaccia into squares.

Braised Caper and Tomato Sauce

3 tomatoes
2 shallots, finely chopped
3 tablespoons capers

1 tablespoon olive oil
1/2 cup red wine
Salt and pepper

1. Wash and core the tomatoes. With a paring knife, mark an X on the bottom of each tomato. Plunge the tomatoes in boiling water for 1 minute or until the skins begin to come off. Transfer the tomatoes to a bowl of ice water. When the tomatoes have cooled completely, peel off their skins and remove their seeds. Coarsely chop the tomatoes.

*Pickled Clams with Tomato and
Oregano Relish on Wonton Chips p. 70*

*Scallop Seviche with Tomato and
Avocado Salsa on Whole Wheat Toasts p. 89*

*Smoked Pheasant with Hummus
on Parmesan Biscuits p. 156*

*Miso Lobster with Endive Chiffonade
in Choux Pastry p. 91*

*Beef Tenderloin with Tomato Caper Relish
on Chili Bagels p. 124*

*Poppy Seed Dusted Sea Bass with
Radish Slaw on Wonton Chips p. 64*

*Oyster, Bacon and Carrot Brochettes
with Caper Tartar p. 68*

*Green Crawfish Cakes Served
with Roasted Red Pepper Aioli p. 80*

Fish Cakes with Tropical Dipping Sauce p. 62

Caramelized Apricot Slices with Camembert on Pumpernickel Toasts p. 23

Roasted Quail with Avocado and Tomato Cream on Tomatillo Tortilla Chips p. 154

Tuna Nori Rolls with Carrot, Radish, Avocado and Tobiko p. 55

Cardamom Scallops with Celeriac Purée on Brown Bread p. 86

Julienne of Chicken Breast with Braised Caper and Tomato Sauce on Fresh Herb Focaccia p. 96

Catfish and Basil Sausages with Cantaloupe Dice on Sesame Pita Chips p. 40

Cajun Smoked Duck Breast with Fennel on Tangy Chive Toasts p. 167

Sliced Rabbit with
Carrot Relish on Rye Toasts p. 158

Cantaloupe and Papaya Slices with
Goat Cheese on Carrot Nut Bread p. 28

Coconut Pork with Basil and
Mango on Parsley Pita Chips p. 140

Marinated Goat Cheese
with Lentil Salad on Andama Toasts p. 14

Sliced Lamb Loin with Oregano Hummus
on Pumpkin Crackers p. 132

Quail Tamales with Tomato
and Avocado Salsa p. 150

Smoked Trout and Tomato Quiches p. 35

Rabbit, Tarragon and Sunflower Seed Terrine
with Glazed Parsnips on Dill Toasts p. 160

Potato Crusted Halibut with
Fennel Relish on Sour Cream Toasts   p. 49

Spicy Turkey Breast with Cantaloupe
on Parmesan Toasts   p. 109

Barbecue Pork with Pineapple Sage Chutney
on Goat Cheese Biscuits   p. 136

Buffalo Patties with Raddichio Sauce
on Cilantro Pita Chips   p. 165

Poached Halibut with Tarragon Sauce
and Lettuce Leaves on Walnut Toasts   p. 47

White Bean, Red Onion and
Basil Stuffed Cherry Tomatoes   p. 16

Anchovy Wrapped Capers with Mozzarella and
Olive Tapenade on Zucchini Slices   p. 34

Prosciutto Stuffed Halibut
with Raddichio on Cornmeal Toasts   p. 51

Roasted Jalapeños with Corn and Cheddar Stuffing p. 17

Miniature Cabbage and Roasted Shallot Quiches p. 12

Split Green Pea Patties with Tomato Yogurt Dipping Sauce   p. 18

Red Cabbage Chiffonade with Apple Chutney and Walnuts on Herb Toasts p. 31

Spinach Rolls with Basil, Mozzarella and Tomato Confit   p. 26

Catfish Nuggets with Raspberry Dipping Sauce p. 39

Clam and Corn Fritters with Blue Cheese and Basil Dressing   p. 74

Crabmeat, Capers and Fennel Stuffed Mushrooms p. 83

Boiled Crawfish with Cantaloupe Papaya Salad
on Sesame Crackers   p. 78

Steamed Mussels with
Cucumber Cardomom Sauce   p. 93

Mahi Mahi with Mango Salsa and
Caper Aioli on Crusty Buttermilk Toasts   p. 58

Oysters Baked on The Half Shell
with Tarragon and Bacon Cream Sauce   p. 66

Basil and Pink Grapefruit Scallops
with Mixed Greens on Anise Crackers   p. 85

Smoked Salmon Cakes   p. 43

Ginger Chicken with Raddichio
and Lentil Salad on Sweet Toasts   p. 102

Beef Tenderloin with Fresh Herb Pesto
on Oregano Biscuits   p. 122

Chicken and Grapefruit Salad in Oat Rolls p. 104

Tarragon Chicken Wings with Caper Mayonnaise p. 106

Sesame and Black Pepper Crusted Beef with Carrot and Endive Slaw on Pita Chips p. 128

Green Peppercorn Crusted Tuna with Wasabi Aioli on Carrot Crackers p. 56

Fresh Herb Pâté with Oregano Mustard on Gouda Thyme Bread p. 145

Skirt Steak Skewers with Mango Salsa p. 118

Chicken Egg Rolls with Apricot Sauce p. 98

Turkey Patties with Tomato Confit and Scallion Aioli on Basil Bagels p. 111

*Turkey Kibbe Kebabs with
Mint Basil Dressing p. 116*

*Fried Quail Legs with
Spicy Lemon Grass Sauce p. 152*

*Braised Beef and Carrots
with Bibb Lettuce in French Rolls p. 126*

*Celeriac Purée with Shiitake Mushrooms
and Rendered Bacon in Phyllo Dough p. 138*

*Pork Tenderloin Stuffed with Sage, Salami,
Asparagus and Roasted Red Peppers p. 142*

Beef, Pecan and Raddichio Strudel p. 119

*Prosciutto and Goat Cheese
Wrapped Cantaloupe Slices p. 139*

*Glazed Shrimp with Oregano Roasted
Shallots on French Bread p. 75*

2. Place the olive oil in a shallow pan over a medium-high heat. When the oil is hot add the shallots. Sauté the shallots for 1 minute. Add the chopped tomatoes to the pan and increase the heat to high. Add the red wine and allow the wine to boil for 1 minute. Decrease the heat to medium-low and continue to simmer the tomatoes, partially covered, for an additional 30 minutes or until the tomatoes have broken up. Add the capers to the tomatoes. Salt and pepper the sauce to one's taste.

Oregano Spread

2 tablespoons cream cheese, softened
6 ounces goat cheese
1 tablespoon sour cream
1/4 cup fresh oregano leaves, finely chopped

Place all of the ingredients in a mixing bowl. Combine the ingredients with a whisk or electric beater.

Julienne of Chicken Breast

1 1/2 pounds boneless chicken breasts
1 teaspoon paprika
1 teaspoon salt
1 garlic clove, peeled and halved
1/4 teaspoon cayenne pepper
2 tablespoons olive oil

1. Rub the chicken breasts with the garlic clove. Combine the paprika, cayenne and salt. Dust the breasts with the spice mixture. In a shallow pan, heat the olive oil over a medium-high heat. When the oil is hot, add the breasts. Cook the breasts for 5-7 minutes on each side or until they are cooked through. Time will vary according to the thickness of the breasts. Cool the breasts and thinly slice them. Toss the strips in the braised caper and tomato sauce.

2. Place 1 teaspoon of oregano spread on a focaccia toast and top it with a few chicken strips. Serve the canapés warm or chilled.

Chicken Egg Rolls with Apricot Sauce

Makes 40 Canapés

Chicken Egg Rolls

Marinade:

1 shallot, finely chopped
2 tablespoons soy sauce
2 parsley sprigs, chopped
1 tablespoon fresh ginger, peeled and chopped
1/4 cup olive oil

3 tablespoons raspberry vinegar
2 garlic cloves, chopped
1 tablespoon black pepper
1 tablespoon lemon juice
1 pound boneless chicken breasts

Egg Rolls:

2 tablespoons olive oil
3 celery stalks, washed and finely chopped
1 Poblano chili, cored, seeded and finely chopped
2 tablespoons rice wine vinegar
2 tablespoons fresh parsley leaves, finely chopped
2 tablespoons fresh cilantro leaves, finely chopped
4 cups canola oil

1 cup shiitake mushrooms, thinly sliced
3 carrots, washed and peeled
1 small daikon, peeled
3 scallions, finely chopped
20 egg roll wrappers
2 eggs

1. In a mixing bowl, combine the shallot, raspberry vinegar, soy sauce, garlic, parsley sprigs, black pepper, ginger, lemon juice and cardamom. Gradually whisk in the olive oil. Pour the marinade over the chicken breasts and refrigerate them overnight.

2. Preheat the oven to 400°F. Strain the chicken breasts and place them in a roasting pan. Roast the breasts for 15 minutes or until they are almost cooked through. Cut the breasts into thin strips and place them in a mixing bowl.

3. In a shallow pan over a medium-high heat, place 1 tablespoon of the olive oil. When the oil is hot, add the mushrooms. Sauté the mushrooms for 10 minutes or until they are wilted. Add the mushrooms to the chicken.

4. In a shallow pan over a medium-high heat, place the remaining olive oil. When the oil is hot, add the celery. Sauté the celery until it is soft, about 10 minutes. Add the celery to the chicken.

5. Slice the carrots and daikon into thin strips and add them to the chicken. Add the Poblano, rice wine vinegar, scallions, parsley and cilantro to the chicken. Incorporate the ingredients thoroughly.

6. Whisk the eggs with 1 tablespoon water. Lay an egg roll wrapper on a flat surface. Place 2 tablespoons of chicken filling near a corner. Fold the nearest corner over the filling. Brush the top edge with some of the egg and water mixture. Forming an envelope, fold the 2 side edges into the center. Roll the wrapper and stuffing into a tight cylinder. Repeat this process with the remaining filling.

7. Place the oil in a pot over a medium-high heat. When the oil reaches 375°F, add a few of the egg rolls. Fry each roll for 4-5 minutes or until it is golden. Transfer the rolls to paper towels to remove any excess grease. Slice the rolls in half.

Apricot Sauce

6 apricots, peeled and pits removed
1 teaspoon rice wine vinegar
2 tablespoons light brown sugar
1 cup red wine

1 tablespoon olive oil
1 tablespoon ginger powder
1 teaspoon green chili paste, optional

1. Coarsely chop the apricots. Place a pot over a medium-high heat. When the pot is hot add the apricots, vinegar, ginger powder, brown sugar and chili paste. Sauté the ingredients until the apricots begin to brown at the edges, about 10 minutes. Add the wine and reduce the heat to medium. Simmer the apricots until they form a mush. In a blender or food processor, purée the apricots until they are smooth. Chill the sauce. Serve the egg rolls warm with the sauce on the side.

Chicken Breast and Carrot Rolls

Makes 40 Canapés

Allspice Glaze

1/2 cup dark brown sugar
1 shallot, chopped
2 tablespoons raspberry vinegar

1 cup red wine
1 tablespoon soy sauce
1/2 teaspoon ground allspice

In a pot, heat the brown sugar and 1/4 cup water over a high heat for 10 minutes. When the sugar reduces down to large bubbles, add the red wine {be very careful of the steam.} Add the chopped shallot, soy sauce, raspberry wine vinegar and the allspice to the wine. Simmer the mixture over a medium-high heat until it is syrupy, about 15 minutes. Cool the glaze.

Carrot stuffing

1 small poblano chili
1 tablespoon unsalted butter
6 ounces Jack cheese

2 carrots
3 green onions

1. Preheat the broiler. Wash the poblano and place it close to the broiler. As the skin blisters turn the poblano, to cook it evenly. When the skin of the chili is completely blistered, place it in a bowl. Cover it tightly with plastic wrap and place the bowl in the refrigerator. Once the poblano is chilled, the skin will peel off easily. Remove as much skin as possible, as well as the seeds and membranes from the poblano. Slice the poblano into thin strips.

2. Wash and peel the carrots. Cut the carrots into very thin strips. In a shallow pan over a medium-high heat, melt the butter. When the butter begins to sizzle, add the carrots and sauté them until they are tender, about 10 minutes. Cool the carrots.

3. Cut the scallions into 1-inch long pieces. Cut the 1-inch long pieces in half, lengthwise. Cut the Jack cheese into thick toothpicks and set them aside.

Chicken Rolls

3 chicken breasts
Salt and pepper

1. Preheat the oven to 350°F. Place a chicken breast in a plastic bag or under plastic wrap. With the smooth side of a mallet or a small pot, pound the breast until it is 1/4- inch thick. Lightly sprinkle the chicken with salt and pepper. Place a few of the scallions, carrots and poblano strips along the longest side of the breast. Place 2 cheese strips on top of the vegetables and roll the breast into a long, tight cylinder. Secure the roll with toothpicks. Repeat this process with the remaining breasts.

2. Generously brush the allspice glaze onto the outside of the chicken rolls. Place the rolls on a baking sheet and into the oven. Cook the chicken for 15 minutes or until cooked through. Slice the rolls into 1/2-inch thick slices. Serve the rolls warm or chilled with toothpicks on the side.

Ginger Chicken with Radicchio and Lentil Salad on Sweet Toasts

Makes 35 Canapés

Sweet Toasts

1 teaspoon dry active yeast
1/4 cup warm water, 105-115°F
1/4 teaspoon baking soda
2 1/2 cups all-purpose flour

1 tablespoon honey
1 cup sour cream, room temperature
1 teaspoon salt
Cornmeal

1. Add the honey to the warm water. Sprinkle the yeast over the warm water. Place the yeast mixture in a warm, draft free area until it is foamy, about 10 minutes.

2. In a bowl, combine the sour cream and baking soda. Add this mixture to the yeast. In a separate bowl, combine the salt and flour. Gradually add the flour to the yeast mixture. Mix the ingredients until a firm dough forms. On a floured surface, knead the dough until it is elastic and smooth, about 10 minutes. Place the dough in an oiled bowl and flip it to oil all sides. Cover the dough and place it in a warm area until it has doubled in bulk.

3. Preheat the oven to 375°F. Generously sprinkle cornmeal on a baking sheet. Gently deflate the dough and form it into two loaves. Place the loaves, seam-sides down, on the baking sheet. Cover the loaves and place them in a warm area, until they have doubled in bulk.

4. Bake the loaves for 25-30 minutes. Allow the loaves to cool completely on a grill.

5. Preheat the broiler. Cut the loaves into 1/2 inch-thick slices. Toast the slices under the broiler until they are lightly brown.

Radicchio and Lentil Salad

1 stalk fresh lemon grass
1/2 cup yellow onion, finely chopped
2 garlic cloves, chopped
1 bay leaf
1 teaspoon ground cumin seed
1 teaspoon ground ginger
Salt and pepper

1 cup lentils
1 carrot, peeled and chopped
2 thyme sprigs
1/2 teaspoon ground cardamom
1 teaspoon chili powder
1 head of raddichio

1. Lay the lemon grass stalk on a cutting board. Cut off the root and discard it. With the smooth side of a mallet or a small pot, pound the white part of the lemon grass until it breaks apart. Finely chop the white part and discard the tough, green stalk.

2. Place the lentils in a pot and cover them with 1 1/2 cups of water. Place the pot over a high heat. Add the onion, carrot, garlic, thyme, bay leaf, cardamom, cumin, chili powder, ginger and lemon grass. When the ingredients boil, reduce the heat to medium. Adding water as needed, simmer the lentils for 20 minutes or until they are tender. Remove the lentils from the heat and discard the thyme and bay leaf. Cool the lentils completely.

3. Remove the coarse outer leaves of the radicchio. Core the radicchio and finely chop the leaves. Toss the radicchio with the lentils and add salt and pepper to taste.

Ginger Chicken

2 tablespoons sesame oil
1 small fresh piece of ginger, peeled
1/4 cup lemon juice

1 pound boneless chicken breasts
Salt and pepper

In a pan, heat the sesame oil over a medium-high heat. Halve the ginger to make two identical pieces. Rub the chicken breasts with the cut side of the ginger. Lightly salt and pepper the breasts. When the oil is hot, place the breasts in the pan and brown them for 8 minutes on each side. Cooking time will vary according to the thickness of the breasts. Cool the chicken and coarsely chop it. Toss the chicken pieces in the lemon juice. Place a spoonful of radicchio and lentil salad on a sweet toast. Top the salad with a few chicken pieces. Repeat this process with the remaining pieces of chicken. Serve the canapés warm or chilled.

Chicken and Grapefruit Salad in Oat Rolls

Makes 40 Canapés

Oat Rolls

1 tablespoon dry active yeast
1 teaspoon granulated sugar
1 1/4 cups warm water, 105-115°F
1 egg, slightly beaten
1 tablespoon unsalted butter, melted
1/4 cup blackstrap molasses
1 1/2 cups oat flour, finely milled
1 1/2 cups all-purpose flour
1 teaspoon salt
Cornmeal

1. Sprinkle the yeast and sugar over 1/2 cup of the warm water. Stir the water until the yeast has dissolved. Allow the yeast to rise in a warm, draft-free area until it is foamy, about 10 minutes.

2. Combine with the yeast mixture the egg, butter, molasses and the remaining water. In a separate bowl, combine the flours and salt. Gradually stir the flours into the yeast mixture until a firm dough forms. On a floured surface, knead the dough until it is smooth and elastic, about 15 minutes. Place the dough in an oiled bowl and flip it to oil all sides. Cover the dough and place it in a warm area. Allow the dough to rise until it has doubled in bulk.

3. Preheat the oven to 350°F. Generously sprinkle cornmeal on a baking sheet. Gently deflate the dough. Split the dough into 40 portions. Shape each portion into a golf ball with a flat bottom. Place the balls on the baking sheets. Bake the rolls for 15-20 minutes or until they are golden brown. Cool the rolls on a grill.

4. Cut the tops off of the rolls. With a melon baller, hollow out the center of each roll.

Chicken Salad

1 tablespoon olive oil
Salt and pepper
1 1/2 pounds boneless chicken breasts
1 tablespoon unsalted butter
1/2 small green cabbage, cored and coarsely chopped
2 carrots, peeled
1 pink grapefruit
1 Poblano chili, cored, seeded and finely chopped
1/2 cup water chestnuts, coarsely chopped

1. In a shallow pan, heat the olive oil over a medium-high heat. Lightly salt and pepper the chicken breasts. When the oil is hot add the breasts. Sear the breasts for 8-10 minutes on each side or until they are cooked through. Cool the breasts and cut them into thin strips.

2. In a pot, melt the butter over a medium-high heat. When the butter begins to sizzle, add the cabbage and cover the pot. Reduce the heat to medium-low. Steam the cabbage for 10 minutes or until it is translucent. Strain and cool the cabbage.

3. With a mandoline or a sharp knife, cut the carrots into thin matchsticks. With a sharp knife, cut the rinds and piths off of the grapefruits. Run the knife along the membranes of the grapefruit, removing the sections. Coarsely chop the grapefruit sections and discard the membranes.

4. In a bowl, combine the chicken, cabbage, carrots, grapefruit sections, Poblano chili and water chestnuts. Toss this mixture in the grapefruit vinaigrette. Place 1 tablespoon of chicken salad in a roll. Repeat this process with the remaining chicken salad. Serve the chilled salad in the warm rolls.

Tarragon Chicken Wings with Caper Mayonnaise

Makes 40 Canapés

Marinade

2 garlic cloves, chopped
1/4 cup fresh tarragon leaves
2 tablespoons lemon juice
1 teaspoon black pepper

1/4 cup chopped yellow onion
1/4 cup red wine vinegar
1 tablespoon Dijon mustard
1/2 cup olive oil

In a blender or food processor, place all of the ingredients except the olive oil. Purée the ingredients until they are smooth. With the machine running, gradually add the olive oil.

Chicken Wings

15 whole chicken wings
2 large eggs
2 cups cracker crumbs, finely ground
1 tablespoon chili powder
4 cups canola oil

2 cups all-purpose flour
2 tablespoons water
1/4 cup cornmeal
1 teaspoon black pepper

1. Lay a chicken wing flat on a cutting board. Cutting at the joint, remove the very thin end wing. Discard this end. Cut the wing at the joint separating the drummette from the middle bone. The drummette is the large bone closest to the breast. The middle appendage has two bones. Remove the smaller of the two bones from the middle appendage. With a sharp knife scrape down the flesh from the top half of the remaining bone. The scraping motion will push the flesh down, forming a ball of chicken meat and skin at the bottom of the bone. Scrape the flesh from the top of the drummette bone in the same manner. The wing pieces should be a ball of flesh with a chicken bone sticking out of the top. Repeat this process with the remaining wings.

2. Place the wings in a shallow pan. Cover the wings with the marinade and refrigerate them overnight.

3. Thoroughly drain the wings. Whisk the egg and water together. Combine the cracker crumbs, cornmeal, chili powder, cumin and pepper. Dredge the wings in the flour. Transfer the wings to the egg wash. After wiping off any excess egg, dredge the wings in the cracker crumb mixture.

4. Place the oil in a pot, over a medium-high heat. When the oil reaches 350°F add a

few of the wings. Fry the wings until they are golden brown and cooked through, about 5-7 minutes each. Transfer the wings to paper towels to remove any excess grease. Repeat this process with the remaining wings.

Caper Mayonnaise

2 large egg yolks
2 teaspoons white vinegar
1 teaspoon white pepper
1/2 cup canola oil
1/4 cup flat leaf parsley leaves, finely chopped
2 tablespoons lemon juice

1 tablespoon Dijon mustard
1 teaspoon salt
1/2 cup olive oil
1/4 cup yellow onion, finely chopped
2 tablespoons capers

In a blender or food processor, place the egg yolks, mustard, vinegar, salt and pepper. Blend the ingredients until they are foamy. With the machine running, add the oils a drop at a time. Transfer the mayonnaise to a mixing bowl and add the onion, parsley, capers and lemon juice. Mix the ingredients thoroughly. Serve the wings warm, with the caper mayonnaise on the side.

Smoked Chicken Salad in Endive Leaves

Makes 30 Canapés

Chicken Marinade

1 small yellow onion, coarsely chopped
1 tablespoon red wine vinegar
1 teaspoon lemon zest
1 teaspoon black pepper
1 pound boneless chicken breasts

3 tablespoons basil, chopped
2 tablespoons lemon juice
1 garlic clove, chopped
1/4 cup olive oil
Maple wood chips

1. In a bowl, whisk together the chopped onion, basil, red wine vinegar, lemon juice, lemon zest, garlic, pepper and olive oil. Pour the marinade over the chicken breasts and marinate them for 6 hours in the refrigerator.

2. Prepare a hot smoker with maple wood chips. Remove the chicken from the marinade. Hot smoke the chicken for 10 minutes. Finish the cooking of the chicken by placing the breasts in a 350°F oven for 10 minutes. Slice the chicken into thin strips.

Salad Dressing

1 poblano chili, cored, seeded and finely chopped
1 tablespoon olive oil
2 tablespoons fresh parsley leaves
1 cup dried apricots, sliced into thin strips
1/4 cup Parmesan cheese, grated

2 shallots, finely chopped
1/4 cup fresh basil leaves
1/2 cup chopped cashews
The leaves of 4 endives, washed
Freshly ground black pepper

1. In a shallow pan over a medium-high heat, place the olive oil. When the oil is hot, add the shallot and poblano chili. Sauté the vegetables until they are tender, about 10 minutes. When the vegetables are tender remove them from the heat. In a blender or food processor, purée the vegetables with the basil and parsley.

2. In a bowl, combine the chili mixture, cashews, dried apricots and the chicken meat. Place 2 tablespoons of the chicken salad on each of the endive leaves. Sprinkle the top with grated Parmesan cheese and freshly ground pepper. Serve the stuffed leaves chilled.

Spicy Turkey Breast with Cantaloupe on Parmesan Toasts

Makes 30 Canapés

Parmesan Toasts

2 cups all-purpose flour
1/2 teaspoon salt
2 tablespoons yellow onion, minced
1/2 teaspoon crushed red pepper
3/4 cup milk

2 teaspoons baking powder
3 tablespoons Parmesan cheese
1/2 teaspoon garlic salt
1/4 cup unsalted butter, melted
1 large egg, beaten

1. Preheat the oven to 400°F. With a fork, combine the flour, baking powder, salt, cheese, onion, garlic salt and crushed red pepper. In a separate bowl, whisk together the butter, milk and egg. With a wooden spoon incorporate the two mixtures. Pour the batter into a well-greased loaf pan and smooth the top. Bake the loaf for 50-60 minutes or until an inserted toothpick comes out clean. Cool the loaf on a grill

2. Preheat the broiler. Cut the loaf into 1/4-inch thick slices. Halve the slices. Toast the slices under the broiler until they are a golden-brown.

Spicy Turkey Breast

2 dried chilies
1 garlic clove
1 tablespoon ground cumin seed
1/4 cup + 2 tablespoons olive oil
salt and pepper

1 red pepper
1 tablespoon ground coriander
2 teaspoons salt
1 pound turkey breast

1. Place the dried chilies in a bowl of warm water for 1 hour.

2. Preheat the broiler. Wash the pepper and place it close to the broiler. Turn the peppers as their skins blister. When the peppers have completely blistered, transfer them to an air-tight container. Seal the container and chill it for 30 minutes. Peel the skins off of the peppers. Remove any seeds or membranes and coarsely chop the peppers.

3. In a blender or food processor, combine the chilies, red pepper, garlic, coriander, cumin and salt. Blend the ingredients until they are smooth. With the machine running, gradually add 1/4 cup of the olive oil.

4. Preheat the oven to 375°F. Rub the turkey breast with 2 tablespoons of olive oil and lightly salt and pepper it. Place the breast in a roasting pan. Roast the turkey breast for 40-45 minutes or until it is cooked through. Cool the turkey breast and slice it into thin strips. Toss the strips in the sauce.

Cantaloupe

1 small cantaloupe
2 scallions, finely chopped
2 tablespoons lime juice

1. Remove the seeds and rind from the cantaloupe. Finely chop the cantaloupe and place it in a mixing bowl. Add the remaining ingredients to the cantaloupe and incorporate them.

2. Place one tablespoon of cantaloupe on a Parmesan toast. Top the cantaloupe with a few turkey slices. Serve the canapés with the turkey meat warm or chilled.

Turkey Patties with Tomato Confit and Scallion Aioli on Basil Bagels

Makes 30 Canapés

Basil Bagels

1/4 cup water
1 tablespoon dry active yeast
1 egg, separated
1 teaspoon salt
2 tablespoons sugar

1/4 cup milk
1 tablespoon unsalted butter, melted
1/4 cup fresh basil leaves, finely chopped
2 cups bread flour

1. Place the water and milk in a pot over a high heat. Heat the liquids to a temperature between 105°F and 115°F. Sprinkle the yeast and sugar over the warm liquid. Allow the yeast to rise in a draft free area for 10 minutes, or until it is foamy.

2. Add the butter, slightly beaten egg white, and basil to the yeast. In a separate bowl, combine the salt and flour. Add the flour to the yeast, 1/2 cup at a time. On a floured surface, knead the dough until it is smooth and elastic, about 15 minutes. Place the dough in a greased bowl and flip it to oil all sides. Cover the dough and allow it to rise in a warm, draft free area until it has doubled in bulk.

3. Gently deflate the dough and divide it into 15 portions. Form each portion into a 2-inch long rope. Brush the ends of the ropes with water and press the ends together, to form a miniature bagel. Cover the bagels with a damp cloth and allow them to rise for 30 minutes, in a warm, draft free area.

4. Preheat the oven to 425°F. Place a large pot of water over a high heat. Add the sugar to the water. When the water boils, reduce the heat to medium. Working in batches, add the bagels to the simmering water. Poach the bagels for 1 minute on each side, or until they are puffy. Place the bagels on a parchment paper lined baking sheet. Brush the bagels with the egg yolk and bake them for 5-10 minutes. Cool the bagels completely.

5. Preheat the broiler. Halve the bagels and toast them under the broiler until they are lightly brown.

Tomato Confit

3 tomatoes
2 garlic cloves, chopped
1 bay leaf
1 tablespoon olive oil

1 shallot, chopped
2 thyme sprigs
1 teaspoon salt

1. Preheat the oven to 250°F. Core the tomatoes. With a paring knife, mark the bottom of each tomato with an X. Plunge the tomatoes in a pot of boiling water for 1 minute or until the skins begin to come off. Transfer the tomatoes to a bowl of ice water. When the tomatoes have cooled completely the skins should peel off easily. Remove the skins and any seeds from the tomatoes.

2. Place the tomatoes, shallots, garlic, thyme and bay leaf in a roasting pan. Sprinkle the salt over the ingredients. Drizzle the olive oil over the ingredients and place the roasting pan in the oven for 30 minutes.

3. Take the roasting pan out of the oven and discard the thyme and bay leaf. Drain the remaining ingredients in a colander for 10 minutes. Coarsely chop the drained ingredients.

Scallion Aioli

2 large egg yolks
2 teaspoons rice wine vinegar
1 teaspoon salt
3 scallions, finely chopped
1/2 cup olive oil

1 tablespoon Dijon mustard
1 teaspoon ground ginger
1/2 teaspoon white pepper
1/2 cup canola oil

In a blender or food processor, place the egg yolks, mustard, vinegar, ginger powder, salt, pepper, and green onions. Blend the ingredients until they are frothy. With the machine running, slowly add the oils. Refrigerate the aioli.

Turkey Patties

2 celery stalks, washed and finely chopped
1/2 cup daikon radish, peeled and finely chopped
1/4 cup fresh sage leaves, finely chopped
1/4 cup fresh parsley leaves, finely chopped
2 garlic cloves, finely chopped
1 teaspoon salt
1 teaspoon black pepper
3 tablespoons Worcestershire sauce
1 pound ground turkey

1. Plunge the celery in a pot of boiling salted water for 5 minutes, or until it is translucent. Transfer the celery to a bowl of ice water. When the celery has cooled, strain it and transfer it to a mixing bowl.

2. Plunge the daikon in a pot of boiling salted water for 5 minutes or until it somewhat soft. Transfer the daikon to a bowl of ice water. When the daikon has cooled, strain it and add it to the celery.

3. Preheat the oven to 375°F. Add the sage, parsley, garlic, salt, pepper, Worcestershire sauce and ground turkey to the celery and daikon. Incorporate the ingredients well. Form 2 tablespoons of the turkey mixture into a small patty. Place the patty on a well-greased baking sheet. Repeat this process with the remaining turkey mixture. Roast the patties for 10-15 minutes or until they are cooked through.

4. Place 1 teaspoon of the tomato confit on a bagel half. Top the tomatoes with a turkey patty. Top the patty with a squirt of scallion aioli. Repeat this process with the remaining patties. Serve the canapés while the patties are still warm.

Smoked Turkey Breast with Sweet Beet Slices on Half-Cracked Black Pepper Crackers

Makes 50 Canapés

Smoked Turkey Breast

1/2 gallon water
1/4 cup bourbon
1/2 teaspoon dried thyme
1 teaspoon juniper berries
1 cup orange juice
2 pounds boneless turkey breast

1/4 pound kosher salt
1/2 cup honey
3 bay leaves
1/2 teaspoon dried sage
1/4 cup fresh ginger, peeled and chopped
Maple wood chips

1. In a large pot combine the water, salt, bourbon, honey, thyme, bay leaves, juniper berries and sage. Bring this mixture to a boil. Boil the ingredients for 5 minutes. Remove the liquid from the heat and add the orange juice and ginger. Cool the liquid completely. When the liquid is cool, add the turkey breast and refrigerate it overnight.

2. Prepare the smoker with maple chips. Drain the turkey breast and hot smoke it for 30 minutes. Transfer the breast to a roasting pan and place it in a 375°F oven to finish the cooking process. The breast should roast about 30-40 minutes, depending on the thickness of the turkey breast. Cool the breast and cut it into thin slices.

Half-Cracked Black Pepper Crackers

2 cups all-purpose flour
1/2 teaspoon baking soda
1/4 cup half-and-half
3 tablespoons cold lard or vegetable shortening cut into small pieces

1/2 teaspoon salt
1 egg, slightly beaten
2 tablespoons half-cracked black pepper

Preheat the oven to 400°F. In a food processor bowl, sift the flour, salt and baking soda. Add the lard pieces. Pulse the mixture until a coarse meal forms. Transfer the flour mixture to a large bowl. Gradually add the egg, half-and-half and the half-cracked black pepper. With a wooden spoon, mix the ingredients until a firm dough forms. On a floured surface, roll out the dough to 1/8th-inch thick. Cut decorative shapes out of the dough and place them on a parchment paper lined baking sheet. Bake the crackers for 7 minutes or until they are lightly brown.

Sweet Beet Slices

3 beets
1 cup raspberry vinegar
1/4 cup sugar

1. Remove the greens from the beets and discard them. Delicately scrub the beets under cold, running water. Plunge the beets in a pot of boiling, salted water. Reduce the heat to medium. Partially cover the pot and simmer the beets for 20 minutes or until they are cooked through. Transfer the beets to a bowl of ice water. When the beets have cooled completely, peel them under running water. Thinly slice the beets.

2. In a shallow pan over a high heat, place the vinegar and the sugar. When the sugar has dissolved, add the beet slices. Toss the beets in the vinegar until they attain an even glaze. Cool the beets completely.

3. Place a few beet slices on a half-cracked black pepper cracker. Top the beets with a slice of turkey breast. Serve the canapés warm or chilled.

Turkey Kibbe Kebabs with Mint Basil Dressing

Makes 50 Canapés

Mint Basil Dressing

2 tablespoons lemon juice
1/4 cup fresh mint leaves, finely chopped
2 cups plain yogurt

2 tablespoons lime juice
1/4 cup fresh basil leaves, finely chopped
2 tablespoons sour cream

Whisk together all of the ingredients. Refrigerate the dressing.

Turkey Kibbe Kebabs

30 wooden skewers, soaked overnight
3 green onions, finely chopped
1 jalapeño, cored, seeded and finely chopped
2 tablespoons chopped parsley leaves
1 teaspoon ground allspice
1/2 teaspoon black pepper
1 cup breadcrumbs
1 tablespoon blackstrap molasses

1 pound ground turkey
1 red pepper, cored, seeded and finely chopped
1 tablespoon plain yogurt
3 tablespoons chopped sage leaves
1/2 teaspoon cayenne pepper
3 tablespoons olive oil
1/4 cup soy
1/2 teaspoon ground cardamom

1. In a food processor, combine the turkey, green onions, red pepper, jalapeño, yogurt, parsley, sage, allspice, cayenne, black pepper and 2 tablespoons of the olive oil. Purée the ingredients until they are smooth. With the machine running, gradually add the breadcrumbs. Refrigerate the mixture for 30 minutes.

2. Preheat the oven to 400°F. Working with wet hands, form 2 tablespoons of turkey mixture around a wooden skewer. Repeat this process with the remaining turkey mixture and chill the skewers for 30 minutes. Place the skewers on a baking sheet. Whisk together the soy, molasses, cardamom and the remaining olive oil. Brush half of the soy mixture onto the kebabs. Place the kebabs in the oven for 10-15 minutes. Brush the remaining soy mixture on the kebabs half way through the cooking process. Serve the kebabs warm with the chilled dressing on the side.

Beef and Lamb

When I was living in Europe, I spent a week trekking through the mountains of Central Greece. It was here that I felt more alienated then ever before. In the desolate villages of Central Greece the people did not understand a word of my native language and I not a word of theirs.

My final dinner was with a few of the curious inhabitants of the village. I tried gesturing and smiling but nothing was expanding my knowledge of the Greek language. Frustrated, we ceased our attempts at communication. The unpleasant silence was broken by the arrival of the main course. A dark-haired woman came from the kitchen with a platter piled high with rosemary crusted lamb chops and small roasted potatoes.

Avoiding any further interlingual conversations, the other diners and I ate. The lamb was the most tender I had ever had. Everyone at the table relaxed as they ate.

The young man to my left tapped my shoulder and pointed to the lamb and then to himself. I gathered the lamb was from his flock. I smiled and patted him on the back in praise. A little girl brought me a sprig of rosemary and said its Greek name for my benefit.

Seeing a possible method of communication, the villagers told me the names of all of the dishes on the table. I pointed to a series of ingredients and then said their English names. Soon we were discussing cuisine by gestures. I learned a few new combinations and recognized some influences from other cultures.

I never had a conversation about politics or the weather with any of the villagers I met but we found a common theme in the versatility of food.

Skirt Steak with Mango Salsa

Makes 30 Canapés

Skirt Steak Skewers

30 wooden skewers, soaked overnight
1 shallot, peeled and finely chopped
1 tablespoon fresh ginger, peeled and minced
1/2 teaspoon ground cardamom
3 tablespoons olive oil
salt and pepper

1 1/2 pounds skirt steak or flank steak
1 garlic clove, peeled and minced
1 teaspoon crushed red pepper
2 tablespoons soy sauce
2 tablespoons sesame oil

1. Cutting across the grain of flesh, slice the skirt steak into 30 2-inch long thin strips. Place the strips in a shallow bowl. Whisk together the shallot, garlic, ginger, crushed red pepper, cardamom, soy sauce, olive oil and 1 tablespoon of the sesame oil. Pour this mixture over the skirt steak. Refrigerate the steak for at least 4 hours.

2. Light your grill or preheat the oven to 400°F. Strain the steak strips and discard the marinade. Thread the steak strips onto the skewers. Lightly salt and pepper the steak strips and place them on a baking sheet. Brush the strips with the remaining sesame oil. Grill the strips for about 5 minutes on each side. This cut of meat is very chewy if underdone, so grill them until they have an even brown crust. If not using your grill, place the strips in the oven for 10 minutes or until they are cooked through. Cover the strips with a towel and keep them in a warm place.

Mango Salsa

2 mangos, peeled, seeded and finely chopped
1/4 cup fresh cilantro leaves, finely chopped
juice of 2 limes

Combine the mango and the cilantro. Sprinkle the lime juice over the mango. Serve the steak strips warm or chilled with the mango salsa on the side.

Beef, Pecan and Radicchio Strudel

Makes 30 Canapés

1 pound flank steak
2 tablespoons olive oil
1 cup pecans, chopped
1 teaspoon salt
1 Radicchio head, cored and finely chopped
1 1/2 cup unsalted butter, melted

Salt and pepper
1/2 cup dry red wine
1/4 cup brown sugar
6 ounces crumbled blue cheese
15 phyllo sheets

1. Cutting across the grain of flesh, slice the flank steak into 1-inch long and 1/2 inch wide pieces. Discard any fat or sinew. Lightly salt and pepper the meat. Place the olive oil in a pan over a medium-high heat. When the oil is hot, add the meat to the pan. Sear the meat so it has a dark exterior but is still very rare, about 3 minutes. Increase the heat to high and add the wine. Cook the meat for an additional 3 minutes. Transfer the meat to a colander. Allow the meat to drain for 10 minutes.

2. Preheat oven to 350°F. Place the brown sugar, salt and 2 tablespoons of water into a shallow pan over high heat. Reduce the liquid until it has big bubbles, about 10 minutes. Add the pecans and stir to completely cover. Transfer the pecans to a baking sheet lined with parchment paper. Place in the oven for 5-7 minutes. This step is to dry out the nuts. Refrigerate the pecans. When cool, shake the baking sheet to separate them.

3. Halve the phyllo sheets length-wise to form 30 3-inch wide and 6-inch long rectangles. When working with the dough, prevent the phyllo from drying out by laying a slightly moist towel over the unused sheets. Lay a phyllo sheet on a flat surface. Brush the sheet with some of the melted butter. Lay another sheet of phyllo on top of the first and brush it with butter. Lay a third sheet of phyllo on the other two. On one of the shorter edges, layer equal amounts of beef, pecans, blue cheese and raddichio. Roll the sheets into a tight cylinder. Brush the end of the sheets with butter and seal the cylinder. Repeat this process with the remaining phyllo sheets. You should have 5 cylinders.

4. Place the cylinders on a parchment paper lined baking sheet and brush them with melted butter. Bake the cylinders for 15 minutes or until they are golden brown. With a serrated knife, slice each roll into 4 slices. Serve the strudels warm.

Beef Tenderloin, Corn Salsa and Jack Cheese Quesadillas

Makes 30 Canapés

Chili Tortillas

1 Dried Poblano chili
1/4 teaspoon baking soda
2 1/2 tablespoons canola oil
1/2 cup plain yogurt
1 cup corn oil
3/4 cups all-purpose flour
1 teaspoon ground cumin seed
1 tablespoon lemon juice
1 teaspoon kosher salt

1. In a spice grinder or food processor, finely grind the dried Poblano chili. In a bowl, combine the flour, baking soda, cumin and ground chili. Gradually whisk in the canola oil. In a separate bowl, combine the lemon juice, yogurt and salt and add it to the flour mixture. Once the ingredients are completely incorporated, knead the dough on a floured surface for 10 minutes. Allow the dough to rest for 30 minutes.

2. Divide the dough into 10 portions. With a tortilla press or a rolling pin, press each portion into a 5-inch wide disc.

Corn Salsa

1 red pepper
2 ears sweet corn
1/2 small red onion, finely chopped
2 tablespoons lime juice
2 tomatoes
1/4 cup curly parsley leaves, finely chopped
2 avocados, peeled, seeded and finely chopped
Salt and pepper

1. Preheat the broiler. Wash the pepper and place it on the top shelf of the oven. As its skin blisters, turn the pepper. When the skin of the pepper has completely blistered, place the pepper in a plastic bag in the refrigerator until completely cool.

2. Wash and core the tomatoes. With a paring knife, mark the bottom of each tomato with an X. Plunge the tomatoes in boiling water for 1 minute or until the skin begins to come off. Transfer the tomatoes to a bowl of ice water. When the tomatoes have completely cooled, take them out of the ice water and peel them. Halve the tomatoes widthwise. Remove the seeds from the tomatoes by squeezing a tomato half. Coarsely chop the tomatoes.

3. Husk the ears of corn and remove any silks. Place the ears in a pot of boiling, salted

water. Cover the pot and cook the ears for 5 minutes. Transfer the ears to a bowl of ice water. When the ears have completely cooled, take them out of the ice water and cut the kernels off of the ears.

4. Remove the skin, seeds and membranes from the roasted red pepper and dice it. In a bowl, mix together the red pepper, tomatoes, corn, parsley, onion, avocados and lime juice. Add salt and pepper to taste.

Beef Tenderloin

1 tablespoon + 1/4 cup corn oil
1 1/2 pounds beef tenderloin
Salt and pepper
1 pound Jack Cheese
Sour Cream

1. Remove any fat or sinew from the beef. Lightly salt and pepper the beef. Place 1 tablespoon of the corn oil in a shallow pan over a medium-high heat. When the oil is hot, add the beef. Brown the beef for 5 minutes on all sides for medium-rare meat. If you desire more cooked beef, lay the beef in a roasting pan and place it in a 400°F oven. Roast the beef for 6 minutes for medium meat and 10 minutes for medium-well meat. Take the meat out of the oven and allow it to rest for 5 minutes before slicing it.

2. Slice the Jack cheese thinly. Cut the beef tenderloin into thin strips. Spread 1/5th of the corn salsa on a tortilla. Top the salsa with slices of Jack cheese. Top the cheese with 1/5th of the beef and then another tortilla. Place a pan over a medium-high heat. When the pan is hot, add 1 tablespoon of the corn oil. When the oil is hot, place the stuffed tortilla in the pan. Cover the pan and reduce the heat to medium. Brown the quesadilla for about 3-5 minutes or until the bottom tortilla is crisp. Flip the quesadilla and cover it. Brown the now bottom quesadilla for about 5 minutes or until the tortilla is crisp and the cheese has melted. Slice the quesadilla into 1/8ths. Adding oil when necessary, repeat this process with the remaining tortillas. Serve the quesadillas warm with sour cream on the side.

Beef Tenderloin with Fresh Herb Pesto on Oregano Biscuits

Makes 35 Canapés

Beef Tenderloin

1 shallot, chopped
2 garlic cloves, chopped
2 tablespoons red wine vinegar
1 teaspoon prepared mustard
1 pound beef tenderloin

2 basil stems, chopped
2 tablespoons balsamic vinegar
1 teaspoon black pepper
1 cup + 1 tablespoon olive oil

1. Whisk together the shallot, basil stems, garlic, balsamic vinegar, red wine vinegar, pepper, mustard and cups of the olive oil. Pour the marinade over the beef and refrigerate it overnight.

2. Preheat the oven to 400°F. Remove the beef from the marinade. Place the remaining olive oil in a shallow pan over a medium-high heat. Lightly salt and pepper the beef and add it to the hot oil. Brown the beef on all sides and transfer it to the oven for 3 minutes. The beef should be medium-rare. If you desire more thoroughly cooked meat, roast the tenderloin 5-7 minutes for medium meat and 11-15 minutes for medium-well meat. These times may vary, depending on the thickness and muscle composition of the meat. Allow the beef to rest for 5 minutes before slicing it.

Oregano Biscuits

1 3/4 cups all-purpose flour
1/2 teaspoon cream of tartar
1/2 cup cold lard or shortening, cut into small pieces

3 teaspoons baking powder
1 tablespoon dried oregano
3/4 cup milk

1. Place the dry ingredients into a food processor. Add the lard pieces. Pulse the mixture until a coarse meal forms, then transfer it to a large bowl. Gradually stir in the milk. Stir this mixture until a firm dough forms. Allow the dough to rest for 30 minutes.

2. Preheat the oven to 375°F. On a floured surface, roll the dough out to 1/2-inch thick. Fold one-half of the dough over the other half, making the dough one-half its original length but double its original thickness. Again, roll the dough out to 1/2-inch thick. Repeat this process 9 more times for a well-layered, flaky dough. Roll the dough 1/2-inch thick. Cut rounds out of the dough and place them on a greased baking sheet. Bake

the biscuits for 10 minutes. Halve the biscuits.

Fresh Herb Pesto

1/4 cup pecans	1/4 cup fresh cilantro leaves
2 tablespoons fresh parsley leaves	1 tablespoon fresh mint leaves
2 tablespoons fresh basil leaves	2 garlic cloves, chopped
1 teaspoon salt	1/2 teaspoon black pepper
3 tablespoons Parmesan cheese, grated	1/4 cup extra-virgin olive oil

In a food processor, place the pecans, cilantro, parsley, mint, basil, garlic, salt, pepper and Parmesan. Purée the ingredients until they are smooth. While the machine is running, gradually add the olive oil. Chill the pesto.

Carrot and Radicchio Julienne

2 carrots, washed and peeled	2 Radicchio heads
1 teaspoon fresh ginger, peeled and minced	1/2 teaspoon ground cumin seed
1/2 teaspoon salt	1/2 teaspoon freshly ground black pepper
3 tablespoons lemon juice	1/4 cup sesame oil

1. Cut the carrots into 2-inch long strips. Halve and core the raddichio. Remove any tough spines from the Radicchio leaves. Slice the leaves into thin strips. In a bowl, whisk together the ginger, cumin, salt, pepper, lemon juice and sesame oil. Toss the carrots and Radicchio in the dressing.

2. Place a small mound of carrots and Radicchio on a biscuit. Top the vegetables with a slice of beef. Squirt 1 teaspoon of pesto onto the beef. Repeat this process with the remaining slices of beef. Serve the canapés warm or chilled.

Beef Tenderloin with Tomato and Caper Relish on Chili Bagels

Makes 30 Canapés

Chili Bagels

1/4 cup water
1 tablespoon dry active yeast
1 egg, separated
1 teaspoon salt
2 tablespoons sugar

1/4 cup milk
1 tablespoon unsalted butter, melted
2 tablespoons dried chili, ground
2 cups bread flour

1. Place the water and milk in a pot over a high heat. Heat the liquids to a temperature between 105°F and 115°F. Sprinkle the yeast and sugar over 1/4 cup of the warm liquid. Allow the yeast to rise in a draft free area for 10 minutes, or until it is foamy.

2. Add the butter, slightly beaten egg white, and chili mixture to the yeast. In a separate bowl, combine the salt and flour. Add the flour to the yeast, 1/2 cup at a time. On a floured surface, knead the dough until it is smooth and elastic, about 10 minutes. Place the dough in a greased bowl and flip it to oil all sides. Cover the dough and allow it to rise in a warm, draft-free area until it has doubled in bulk.

3. Gently deflate the dough and divide it into 15 portions. Form each portion into a 2-inch long rope. Brush the ends of the ropes with water and press the ends together, to form a miniature bagel. Cover the bagels with a damp cloth and allow them to rise for 30 minutes, in a warm, draft-free area.

4. Preheat the oven to 425°F. Place a large pot of water over a high heat. Add the sugar to the water. When the water boils, reduce the heat to medium. Working in batches, add the bagels to the simmering water. Poach the bagels for 1 minute on each side, or until they are puffy. Place the bagels on a parchment paper lined baking sheet. Brush the bagels with the egg yolk and bake them for 5-10 minutes. Cool the bagels completely.

5. Preheat the broiler. Halve the bagels and toast them under the broiler until lightly browned.

Tomato Caper Relish

4 tomatoes
2 garlic cloves, minced
2 tablespoons olive oil
1 teaspoon freshly ground black pepper
1 shallot, chopped
2 parsley stems
4 tablespoons capers

1. Core the tomatoes. With a paring knife, mark the bottom of each tomato with an X. Plunge the tomatoes in a pot of boiling water for 1 minute, or until their skins begin to come off. Transfer the tomatoes to a bowl of ice water. When the tomatoes have completely cooled, remove them from the water and peel them. Cut the tomatoes into quarters. Remove the seeds and membranes from the quarters.

2. Preheat the oven to 250°F. Place the tomato quarters, shallot, garlic and parsley stems in a roasting pan. Drizzle the olive oil over the tomatoes. Roast the tomatoes for 30 minutes. Discard the parsley stems.

3. Finely chop the tomatoes and place them in a mixing bowl. Add the capers and pepper to the tomatoes and blend thoroughly. Chill the relish.

Beef Tenderloin Slices

6 tablespoons olive oil
Salt and pepper
2 tablespoons balsamic vinegar
1 shallot, chopped
1 1/4 pounds beef tenderloin
1/4 cup fresh basil leaves, chopped
2 garlic cloves, chopped
1 tablespoon Worcestershire

1. Preheat the oven to 400°F. Remove the beef from the marinade. Place 1 tablespoon of olive oil in a shallow pan over a medium-high heat. Lightly salt and pepper the beef and add it to the hot oil. Brown the beef on all sides and transfer it to the oven for 3 minutes. The beef should be medium-rare. If you desire more thoroughly cooked meat, roast the tenderloin 5-7 minutes for medium meat and 11-15 minutes for medium-well meat. These times vary, depending on the thickness and muscle composition of the meat. Allow the beef to rest for 5 minutes before slicing it.

2. In a mixing bowl, place the basil, vinegar, garlic, shallot and Worcestershire. Gradually whisk in the remaining olive oil. Set the dressing aside.

3. Cutting across the grain of flesh, thinly slice the beef. Place 1 tablespoon of relish on a chili bagel. Top the relish with a slice of beef tenderloin. Drizzle 1 teaspoon of dressing over the beef. Repeat this process with the remaining slices of beef tenderloin. Serve the canapés with the beef warm or chilled.

Braised Beef and Carrots with Bibb Lettuce in French Rolls

Makes 40 Canapés

French Rolls

1 tablespoon dry active yeast
1 teaspoon granulated sugar
1 cup warm water, 105-115°F
3 cups all-purpose flour
1 tablespoon salt
Cornmeal

1. In a large bowl, sprinkle the yeast and sugar over 1/2 cup of the warm water. Allow the yeast to rise in a warm, draft free area until it is foamy, about 10 minutes.

2. Add the remaining water to the yeast. In a separate bowl, combine the flour and salt. Gradually stir the flour into the yeast until a shaggy dough forms. On a floured surface, knead the dough for 10 minutes, or until it is smooth and elastic. Place the dough in an oiled bowl and flip it to oil all sides. Cover the dough and allow it to rise in a warm area until it has doubled in bulk.

3. Generously sprinkle cornmeal on a baking sheet. Gently deflate the dough. Shape the dough into 40 golf-balls with flat bottoms. Place the balls on the baking sheet. Place the baking sheet in a cold oven. Set the oven temperature at 400°F and bake the rolls for 15-20 minutes or until golden brown. Cool the rolls on a grill.

4. Slice the tops off of the rolls and hollow them out with a melon baller.

Braised Beef and Carrots

1 large tomato
2 pounds chuck beef
3 carrots, peeled
2 tablespoons olive oil
2 shallots, chopped
Salt and pepper
1 cup red wine
1 cup low sodium chicken stock or water
1/4 cup all-purpose flour
1 head of Bibb Lettuce, ripped into small leaves

1. Core the tomato. With a paring knife, mark the bottom of the tomato with an X. Plunge the tomato in a pot of boiling water for 1 minute, or until the skin begins to peel off. Transfer the tomato to a bowl of ice water. When the tomato has completely cooled, remove the skin and seeds. Coarsely chop the tomato.

2. Cut the beef into small cubes. Finely chop the carrots. Place the olive oil in a dutch oven over a medium-high heat. Lightly salt and pepper the pieces of beef. When the oil is hot, add the beef. Brown the beef on all sides. Add the carrots and shallots to the dutch oven and cook them for 5 minutes.

3. Preheat the broiler. Add the wine to the dutch oven. Allow the wine to boil for 30 seconds. Add the stock and the tomatoes to the dutch oven. Sift the flour over the meat and place it under the broiler for 2 minutes or until the flour is lightly brown. Whisk in the flour. Place the pot over a medium-low heat and cover it. Lightly simmer the meat for 1 hour or until the meat is tender.

4. Place a leaf of Bibb lettuce in a roll. Fill the roll with meat and carrots. Serve while the meat is still warm.

Sesame and Black Pepper Crusted Beef with Carrot and Endive Slaw on Pita Chips

Makes 40 Canapés

Pita Chips

1 teaspoon dry active yeast
1/2 cup warm water, 105-115°F
1 tablespoon ground ginger
1/2 teaspoon salt

1 teaspoon sesame oil
1 teaspoon honey
1 1/2 cups bread flour

1. Whisk together the yeast, sesame oil, warm water, honey and ginger. In a separate bowl, combine the flour and salt and add them to the yeast mixture. Stir the mixture with a wooden spoon until a firm dough forms. On a floured surface, knead the dough until it is smooth and elastic, about 10 minutes. Place the dough in an oiled bowl and flip it to oil all sides. Cover the bowl with a towel and place it in a warm place. Allow the dough to rise until it has doubled in bulk.

2. Gently deflate the dough and divide it into 5 portions. Let the portions rest for 10 minutes.

3. Preheat the oven to 500°F. Place a baking sheet in the oven. Working with one's palm on a floured surface, form each portion of dough into a 1/4-inch thick round. Rest the rounds for 10 minutes. Place the rounds on the heated baking sheet and bake them until they puff up and brown, about 3 minutes on each side.

4. Peel the two layers of a pita in half to form 2 separate rounds. Cut the rounds into triangles. Toast the triangles until crisp.

Carrot and Endive Slaw

2 carrots, peeled
2 tablespoons lemon juice
2 tablespoons sesame oil
3 scallions, green parts only, sliced into 1-inch long strips
1 tablespoon fresh ginger, peeled and finely chopped

2 endive heads
2 tablespoons rice wine vinegar
3 tablespoons extra virgin olive oil

Slice the carrots into thin strips. Remove the outer leaves from the endive. Halve the endive and remove the core. Slice the endive lengthwise into thin strips. Combine the carrots, endive and scallions. In a separate bowl, combine the lemon juice, ginger, vinegar and sesame oil. Pour the dressing over the carrots and endive and toss them to coat.

Sesame and Black Pepper Crusted Beef

3 tablespoons white sesame seeds
2 tablespoons half-cracked black pepper
2 tablespoons olive oil

1 1/2 pounds beef tenderloin
1 tablespoon salt

1. Place a pan over a high heat. When the pan is hot add the sesame seeds. Toss the seeds in the pan until they are toasted. Cool the seeds.

2. Remove any fat or nerves from the beef tenderloin. Cut the beef tenderloin into 2-inch thick pieces. Combine the sesame seeds, half-cracked black pepper and salt. Press each side of a beef piece in the spice mixture. Place one tablespoon of the olive oil in a pan over a medium-high heat. When the oil is hot add half of the beef. Cook the strips for 3 minutes on each side, or until they are nice and brown. Repeat this process with the other half of beef, adding oil as needed. Allow the meat to sit for 3 minutes before slicing it.

3. Cutting across the grain of the flesh, thinly slice the beef. Place a bed of carrot and endive slaw on a pita chip. Top the slaw with a piece of sesame and black pepper crusted beef. Repeat this process with the remaining slices of beef. Serve these canapés warm or chilled.

Mint Pesto Stuffed Lamb with Shaved Fennel

Makes 40 Canapés

Mint Pesto

1/2 cup fresh basil leaves
2 garlic cloves, finely chopped
1 teaspoon salt
1/4 cup Parmesan cheese, grated

1/4 cup fresh mint leaves
1/4 cup pine nuts
1 teaspoon black pepper
1/2 cup bread crumbs

In a food processor, place the basil, mint, garlic, pine nuts, salt, pepper and Parmesan cheese. With the machine running, gradually add the remaining olive oil. Stir in the bread crumbs. Chill the pesto.

Stuffed Loin of Lamb

1 pound lamb loin or 2 1/2 pound loins
1 teaspoon black pepper
1 tablespoon soy sauce

2 tablespoons balsamic vinegar
1 garlic clove, finely chopped
1/4 cup olive oil

1. With a long, thin knife make an incision in the center of the lamb loin, forming a tunnel through the loin. Combine the balsamic vinegar, black pepper, garlic, soy and olive oil. Pour the marinade over the loin and marinate the loin overnight.

2. Preheat the oven to 350°F. Take the loin out of the marinade and pat it dry. With a pastry bag, pipe the pesto into the loin. Use toothpicks to close up each end. The pesto will run out if the holes are left open. In a pan, heat 1 tablespoon of the olive oil over a high heat. When the oil is hot, add the loin. Brown the loin for 3-4 minutes on each side. Place the loin into the oven for 5 minutes for medium-rare meat. You may roast the loin for longer, depending on the meat's thickness and how you like it. Allow the loin to rest for 5 minutes before slicing. Remove the toothpicks and cut the loin into 1/2-inch thick slices.

Croutons

1 tablespoon dry active yeast
1/4 cup heavy whipping cream
1 teaspoon salt
1 tablespoon ground mustard powder
1 egg white beaten with 1 tablespoon cold water

1 cup warm water, 105-115°F
2 cups all-purpose flour
1 tablespoon granulated sugar
3 tablespoons shortening or butter, melted

1. Sprinkle the yeast over the warm water and let it rise for 10 minutes in a warm place.

2. Scald the cream. Combine the cream with the yeast mixture. In a separate bowl, combine the flour, salt, half of the sugar and ground mustard. Form these ingredients into a well. In a bowl combine the cream, melted shortening and the remaining sugar. In the center of the well add the yeast and the cream mixtures. Gradually combine the wet and dry ingredients until a firm dough has formed. Without kneading the dough, place it in an oiled bowl and flip it to oil all sides. Allow the dough to rise in a warm place until it has doubled in size.

3. Gently deflate the dough. With a rolling pin, roll the dough out to a 1/8th-inch thick rectangle. Beginning at one of the longer edges, roll the dough into a cylinder. Cut four 1/8th-inch deep slits into the top of the loaf. Let the dough rise in a warm place until it has almost doubled in size.

5. Preheat the oven to 400°F. Place a pan filled with water on the bottom rack of the oven. Bake the dough for 15 minutes. Reduce the temperature to 350°F and bake the dough for an additional 30 minutes. Brush the egg white and water on the loaf and bake the bread an additional 5 minutes. Cool the loaf on a grill.

6. Preheat the broiler. Slice the loaf into 1/4-inch thick slices. Toast the slices under the broiler until they are golden.

Shaved Fennel

2 tablespoons extra-virgin olive oil
1/2 red onion, finely chopped
1 tomato, deseeded and finely chopped

1 tablespoon balsamic vinegar
1 fennel head
1 teaspoon coarsely ground black pepper

1. Whisk together the vinegar and olive oil. Pick 1/4 cup of fennel fronds off of the fennel stalks. Finely chop the fronds. Remove the stalks. Half the fennel and cut out the core. With a very sharp knife or a mandoline, cut the fennel into paper thin slices. In a bowl, combine the fennel, tomato, onion and fronds. Pour the vinaigrette and pepper over the vegetables and toss the vegetables to coat.

2. Place 1 tablespoon of the shaved fennel on the croutons. Top with a slice of warm lamb. These canapés are great warm or chilled.

Sliced Loin of Lamb with Oregano Hummus on Pumpkin Crackers

Makes 40 Canapés

Marinated Lamb

1 1/2 pounds lamb loin
6 tablespoons olive oil
2 garlic cloves, chopped
3 tablespoons fresh mint leaves, chopped
1 tablespoon fresh ginger, peeled and chopped
2 tablespoons sesame oil

salt and pepper
1 shallot, coarsely chopped
2 tablespoons fresh thyme leaves
3 tablespoons raspberry vinegar
1 teaspoon black pepper

1. Preheat oven to 400°F. Remove any fat or gristle from the lamb loin. Lightly salt and pepper the loin. In a shallow pan, heat 1 tablespoon of the olive oil over a medium-high heat. When the oil is hot, add the lamb loin. Brown the loin for 3 minutes on all sides. Place the loin in the oven for 5 minutes for medium-rare meat and 10 minutes for medium meat, depending on the thickness of the meat. Take the lamb loins out of the oven and let it rest for 5 minutes before slicing.

2. In a blender or food processor, place the shallot, garlic, thyme, mint, vinegar, ginger and pepper. Blend the ingredients until they are completely incorporated. While the machine is running, gradually add the sesame oil and the remaining olive oil.

3. Thinly slice the lamb and place it in a shallow bowl. Pour the marinade over the lamb slices and chill them for 1 hour.

Pumpkin Crackers

4 ounces canned, cooked pumpkin flesh
2 cups all-purpose flour
3/4 teaspoon baking soda
1 egg, slightly beaten

2 tablespoons water
1 teaspoon salt
2 tablespoons lard or vegetable shortening
1/4 cup buttermilk

1. In a pot, heat the pumpkin flesh with the water. When the pumpkin flesh is hot, strain it and reserve 3 tablespoons of the juice.

2. Combine the flour, salt, baking soda and the shortening. Rub these ingredients between one's hands or pulse them in a food processor, until they form a coarse meal. Add the egg, buttermilk and pumpkin juice to the flour and butter mixture. Mix until

a firm dough forms. Refrigerate the dough for 20 minutes before rolling.

3. Preheat the oven to 400°F. On a lightly floured surface, roll the dough 1/4-inch thick. Cut shapes out of the dough and place them on a greased baking sheet. Bake the crackers for 5-7 minutes or until they are crisp.

Oregano Hummus

1 red pepper	2 cups cooked chic peas, rinsed if canned
1/4 cup fresh oregano leaves	2 garlic cloves, chopped
1 tablespoon tahini	2 tablespoons lemon juice
1 teaspoon salt	1/4 cup olive oil

1. Preheat the broiler. Wash the red pepper and place it under the broiler. Turn the pepper to roast all sides. When the skin of the pepper has completely blistered, place the pepper in an air-tight container and chill it.

2. Place in a blender or food processor, the chic peas, oregano, garlic, tahini, lemon juice and salt. Blend the ingredients until they are smooth. While the machine is running, slowly add the olive oil. The Hummus should be smooth.

3. Remove the skin, seeds and membranes from the red pepper. Finely chop the pepper and fold it into the Hummus.

4. Strain the lamb slices. Place 1 teaspoon of Hummus on a pumpkin cracker. Top the Hummus with a slice of lamb. Repeat this process with the remaining slices of lamb. Serve the canapés chilled.

Pork

My roommates had always eaten extremely well. One would suffer stomachaches if she ate a meal I did not prepare. In return, they paid half of a sizeable grocery bill and had relinquished any and all privileges to the kitchen.

Upon planning a week-long trip with my family, my roommate became giddy with excitement. "I can't wait to get back in the kitchen for a week," she said. "I haven't cooked in so long. I got some recipes from my mother to refresh my memory. I can prepare them and then freeze them for a later date." After, she reeled off the names of a few casseroles, she came to her favorite frozen entrée. "Ham sandwiches," she said proudly. I giggled thinking that the only cooking she'd be doing would involve a phone and a delivery menu.

Upon my return home, I opened the refrigerator and was surprised to find not one pizza box. My astonishment increased when I opened the freezer door. I found it filled with ham sandwiches wrapped in aluminum foil.

Barbecue Pork with Pineapple Sage Salsa on Goat Cheese Biscuits

Makes 30 Canapés

Goat Cheese Biscuits

2 cups all-purpose flour
2 teaspoons light brown sugar
1/4 teaspoon garlic salt
1 teaspoon ground cumin seed
1/2 cup cold lard or shortening, cut into small pieces
1 cup milk

1 teaspoon baking powder
1/2 teaspoon cream of tartar
1 tablespoon chili powder

6 ounces goat cheese

1. In a food processor bowl, combine the sifted flour, baking powder, brown sugar, cream of tartar, garlic powder and cumin. Add the pieces of lard and pulse until it resembles a coarse meal. Transfer the mixture to a large bowl and crumble in the goat cheese. Gradually stir in the milk until a firm dough forms. Allow the dough to rest for 30 minutes.

2. Preheat the oven to 375°F. On a floured surface, roll the dough into a 1/2-inch thick rectangle. Fold one-half of the dough over the other half, making the dough 1/2 its original length but double its original thickness. Again, roll the dough out to 1/2-inch thick. Repeat this process 9 more times for a flaky dough. Roll the dough 1/2-inch thick. Dust a small round cutter with flour. Cut small rounds out the dough. Place the rounds on a well-greased baking sheet. Bake the biscuits for 10 minutes or until they are lightly brown. Cool the biscuits on a grill. When the biscuits have cooled, halve them.

Barbecue Pork

1 tablespoon unsalted butter
1 pound pork shoulder or butt, cut into 1-inch cubes
2 jalapeños, cored, seeded and finely chopped
1 tablespoon dark chili powder
1/2 cup cider vinegar
1/2 cup Worcestershire sauce
Salt and pepper
1 yellow onion, finely chopped
2 garlic cloves, finely chopped
1 tablespoon tomato paste
1/2 cup dark brown sugar
2 tablespoons fresh oregano leaves, finely chopped

1. In a deep pan, melt half of the butter over a medium-high heat. Lightly salt and pepper the pork cubes. When the butter begins to sizzle, add the pork cubes to the pan. Brown the pork on all sides, about 5 minutes. Using a slotted spoon transfer the pork to paper towels, hereby removing any excess grease. Add the onion, jalapeños, garlic, chili powder and the remaining butter to the pan. Reduce the heat to medium. Scrape the bottom of the pan with a wooden spoon, to release all of the brown bits. Sauté the ingredients until the onions are golden. In a bowl, whisk together the vinegar, tomato paste and brown sugar. Add the liquid to the pan. Add the Worcestershire and the pork pieces to the pan. Cover the pan and reduce the heat to low. Lightly simmer the meat for 45 minutes or until it is very tender.

2. When the meat is easily shredded, remove the pork pieces with a slotted spoon. Increase the heat to medium-high and rapidly simmer the sauce until it acquires a syrupy consistency. Shred the pork meat by dragging the back of a fork across individual cubes until they break apart. Add the meat and the oregano to the sauce and store it over a low heat.

Pineapple Sage Salsa

1 pineapple, peeled, cored and cut into small cubes
1/4 cup fresh sage leaves
2 tablespoons rice wine vinegar

1. Combine all of the ingredients. Allow the ingredients to marinate for 30 minutes.

2. Place 1 tablespoon of Barbecue pork on the half of a biscuit. Top the pork with 1 teaspoon of pineapple sage chutney. Repeat this process with the remaining pork. Serve while the pork is still warm.

Celeriac Purée with Shiitake Mushrooms and Rendered Bacon in Phyllo Dough

Makes 40 Canapés

1 head of celeriac
1 pound lean bacon, coarsely chopped
2 cups shiitake mushrooms, stems removed and finely chopped
1/2 cup Jarlsberg cheese, grated
2 teaspoons salt
1 1/2 cups unsalted butter, melted
2 cups milk
1 tablespoon olive oil
1 teaspoon white pepper
15 phyllo sheets

1. Peel the celeriac and cube it. Place the celeriac and the milk in a small pot. If there is not enough milk to completely cover the celeriac, add water. Place the pot over a medium-high heat. Simmer the celeriac for 30 minutes or until it is tender. Strain the celeriac and place it in a food processor. Purée the celeriac until it is smooth. Place the purée in a mixing bowl.

2. Place the bacon in a shallow pan over a medium heat. Stirring the bacon often, cook it until it is crispy, about 15 minutes. With a slotted spoon, transfer the bacon to paper towels to remove any excess grease. Add the bacon to the celeriac.

3. In a shallow pan over a medium-high heat, place the olive oil. When the oil is hot, add the shiitake mushrooms. Sauté the mushrooms until they are soft, about 10 minutes. Add the mushrooms to the celeriac.

4. Add the Jarlsberg cheese, pepper and salt to the celeriac mixture. Incorporate the ingredients well.

5. Lay a phyllo sheet on a flat surface. Cover the remaining sheets with a slightly damp towel. Brush melted butter on the phyllo sheet and fold it in half. Brush the sheet with more butter and fold it in half again to form a long rectangle. Place 2 tablespoons of the celeriac filling on one of the shorter edges. Forming a triangle, fold the edge of the phyllo dough over the filling. Fold the filling and phyllo dough as one would a flag. The result should be a triangle with no filling showing. Place the triangle on a non-stick baking sheet. Repeat this process with the remaining filling. At this point the phyllo triangles can be frozen for up to one week. Allow them to defrost completely before cooking.

6. Preheat the oven to 350°F. Brush the triangles with the remaining melted butter. Place the triangles in the oven and bake them until the phyllo dough is golden and flaky, 10-15 minutes. Halve the triangles and serve them warm.

Prosciutto and Goat Cheese Wrapped Cantaloupe Slices

Makes 30 Canapés

30 Prosciutto slices
30 basil leaves
8 ounces goat cheese
30 1-inch long cantaloupe pieces

Place 1 teaspoon of goat cheese on each end of the Prosciutto. Top the goat cheese with a basil leaf and then a cantaloupe piece. Roll the Prosciutto around the cantaloupe. Repeat this process with the remaining ingredients. Serve the rolls at room temperature.

Coconut Pork with Basil and Mango on Pita Chips

Makes 40 Canapés

Parsley Pita Chips

1 teaspoon dry active yeast
1/2 cup warm water, 105-115°F
1/2 cup fresh parsley leaves, finely chopped
1/2 teaspoon salt

1 teaspoon olive oil
1 teaspoon honey
1 1/2 cups bread flour

1. Whisk together the yeast, olive oil, warm water, honey and parsley. In a separate bowl, combine the flour and salt and add them to the yeast mixture. Stir the mixture with a wooden spoon until a firm dough forms. On a floured surface, knead the dough until it is smooth and elastic, about 10 minutes. Place the dough in an oiled bowl and flip it to oil all sides. Cover the bowl with a towel and place it in a warm place. Allow the dough to rise until it has doubled in bulk.

2. Gently deflate the dough and divide it into 5 portions. Let the portions rest for 10 minutes.

3. Preheat the oven to 500°F. Place a baking sheet in the oven. Working with one's palm on a floured surface, form each portion of dough into a 1/2-inch thick round. Rest the rounds for 10 minutes. Place the rounds on the hot baking sheet and bake them until they puff up and brown, about 3 minutes on each side.

4. Peel the two layers of a pita in half to form 2 separate rounds. Quarter the rounds and toast them until golden.

Coconut Pork

1 1/2 pounds pork loin
1 yellow onion, finely chopped
2 jalapeños, cored, seeded and finely chopped
1 tablespoon ground turmeric
1 teaspoon salt
1/2 cup half-and-half
2 thyme sprigs

2 tablespoons olive oil
6 garlic cloves, minced
1 tablespoon ground coriander
1/2 teaspoon ground ginger
1 cup coconut milk
2 bay leaves

1. Trim any excess fat or nerves from the pork loin. Cut the loin into 1-inch cubes. Place the olive oil in a deep pan or wok over a high heat. When the oil is hot, add the onion and garlic. Reduce the heat to medium-high. Sauté the onion until it is golden,

about 10 minutes. Add the jalapeños, coriander, turmeric, ginger and salt to the pan. Sauté the ingredients until the Jalapeños are tender, about 10 minutes. Add the pork pieces to the pan. Sear the pork on all sides Add the coconut milk, half-and-half, bay leaves and thyme. Simmer the ingredients until the sauce covers a spoon and the pork is tender, about 15 minutes. Remove the bay leaf and thyme from the pan. Keep the pork and the sauce warm.

Basil and Mango

1 cup orange juice
2 tablespoons light brown sugar
1/2 red onion, finely chopped
1 tablespoon lime zest, chopped

2 tablespoons lime juice
1 mango, peeled, seeded and finely chopped
1 tablespoon orange zest, chopped
3 tablespoons fresh basil leaves, chopped

1. Place the orange juice, lime juice and brown sugar in a small pot over a high heat. Boil the juices until the sugar has dissolved. Cool the mixture.

2. In a bowl combine the mango, onion, orange zest, lime zest and basil. Toss the mango mixture with the cooled juice mixture.

3. Spread the basil and mango on a pita chip. Top with a piece of pork and some sauce. Serve immediately. Make only as many as you'll need, as the sauce will make the pita soggy.

Pork Tenderloin Stuffed with Sage, Salami, Asparagus and Roasted Red Peppers

Makes 35 Canapés

1 red pepper
4 asparagus spears
2 pounds pork tenderloin
6 Salami slices
4 ounces Gouda cheese, cut into 1/2-inch thick strips
1/4 cup fresh sage leaves, finely chopped

1. Preheat the broiler. Wash the red pepper. Place the red pepper close to the broiler. Turn the pepper as its skin blisters. When the pepper is completely blistered, transfer it to an airtight container. Seal the container and chill it. When the pepper is cool, peel it and remove any seeds or membranes. Cut the pepper into quarters.

2. Snap the woody ends off of the asparagus. Plunge the asparagus spears in a pot of boiling, salted water for 2 minutes. You don't need to cook them completely. Transfer the spears to a bowl of ice water. When the spears have cooled completely drain them.

3. Trim all nerves and any excess fat from the tenderloin. Make an incision, lengthwise, down the center of the tenderloin. The incision should cut through two-thirds of the tenderloin and form a bulge of flesh on each side of the tenderloin. Make a similar incision in each of the bulges, cutting only two-thirds into each side. The result should be a rectangle that is four times the original width of the tenderloin.

4. Preheat the oven to 375°F. Spread the tenderloin out flat. Cover it with plastic wrap. With the smooth side of a mallet or a small pot, pound the tenderloin until it is 1/2-inch thick. Layer the Salami slices along the length of the tenderloin. Top the salami with the red peppers. Place the asparagus spears on top of the peppers with the ends touching each other and the tips sticking out. On either side of the spears, place strips of the Gouda. Sprinkle the sage over the ingredients. Beginning at one of the wider ends, roll the tenderloin into a tight cylinder. Secure the tenderloin with toothpicks or butcher twine. Place the tenderloin in a roasting pan and roast it for 20 minutes. Flip the tenderloin and roast it for an additional 15 minutes. Remove the toothpicks or twine and cut the tenderloin into 1/4-inch thick slices. Serve the slices warm or chilled.

Asparagus, Basil, Mozzarella and Serrano Ham Rolls

Makes 35 Canapés

80 thin asparagus spears
20 basil leaves or about 1/4 pound
10 ounces fresh mozzarella
20 thin slices of Serrano Ham(prosciutto may be substituted)
3 tablespoons olive oil

1. Snap the woody stems off of the asparagus. Plunge the spears into a pot of boiling salted water for 3-5 minutes or until they are cooked through. Transfer the spears to ice water and cool completely. Drain completely.

2. Slice the mozzarella into thick toothpicks. Lay a slice of ham on a flat surface. Line two basil leaves on one of the shorter ends of a ham slice. Top the basil with two asparagus spears. Layer 2 pieces of mozzarella on the spears and top with two additional asparagus spears. Roll the ham around the ingredients to form a tight roll with the asparagus tips poking out of the top. Repeat this process with the remaining ham.

3. Place a pan over high heat. When the pan is hot add 1 tablespoon of the olive oil. Working in 3 batches, place a few of the rolls into the hot oil. If you crowd the pan you will slow the cooking process. Getting the ham as crispy as possible without burning, brown the rolls on all sides. Repeat this process with the remaining rolls, adding olive oil as needed. These are great hot but also good chilled or at room temperature.

Cantaloupe and Papaya Salad with Prosciutto in Plums

Makes 40 Canapés

1/4 cup fresh basil leaves, finely chopped
1 tablespoon orange zest
2 tablespoons lime juice
2 tablespoons poppy seeds
1 tablespoon rice wine vinegar
2 tablespoons extra virgin olive oil
1 tablespoon sesame oil
1 small cantaloupe
2 papayas
1 pound prosciutto, thinly sliced
20 plums

1. In a bowl, whisk together the basil, orange zest, lime juice, poppy seeds, rice wine vinegar, olive oil and sesame oil. Peel and seed the cantaloupe and papaya. Finely chop the fruit. Pour the marinade over the fruit and let it sit for 15 minutes at room temperature.

2. Slice the prosciutto into thin strips. Cutting around the pit, halve each plum. Add half the prosciutto strips to the fruit salad. Fill each of the plums with 1 tablespoon of the fruit salad. Garnish with extra prosciutto strips.

Fresh Herb Pâté with Oregano Mustard on Gouda-Thyme Bread

Makes 45 Canapés

Fresh Herb Pâté

1 pound veal, cubed
1/2 pound chicken livers, trimmed and chopped
5 thyme sprigs
1/2 teaspoon cayenne pepper
1/2 yellow onion, finely chopped
2 garlic cloves, chopped
1 cup port wine
2 tablespoons fresh parsley leaves, chopped
Boiling water

2 pounds pork butt, cubed
3 bay leaves
2 1/2 teaspoons salt
1/2 teaspoon black pepper
3 celery stalks, washed and finely chopped
1/2 cup brandy
2 egg whites
1/4 cup fresh oregano leaves, chopped

1. In a bowl, combine the veal, pork butt, chicken livers, bay leaves and thyme sprigs. In a separate bowl, whisk together the salt, cayenne pepper, black pepper, onion, celery, garlic, brandy and port. Pour the marinade over the meat and allow this mixture to marinate for 24 hours.

2. Remove the bay leaves and thyme sprigs and strain the meat in a colander for 30 minutes. Preheat the oven to 300°F. Place the strained meat and vegetables in a food processor. Purée the mixture until it is smooth, you may have to work in batches. With the machine running, add the egg whites, parsley and oregano and purée the meat for an additional 30 seconds. Place the mixture into a well-greased porcelain mold and smooth the top. Place 2 layers of paper towels on the bottom of a roasting pan. Place the porcelain mold in the center of the roasting pan. Fill the roasting pan with enough boiling water to reach 2/3rds the height of the mold. Place the roasting pan in the oven for 1 1/2 hours. Weight the pâté with an aluminum foil-wrapped brick and continue the cooking process for an additional hour. Cool the pâté in its mold for at least 6 hours. After running a knife along the edges of the mold, turn the mold over onto a flat surface. Slice the pâté into 1/2-inch thick slices.

Gouda-Thyme Bread

1/4 cup unsalted butter, melted
1 egg, beaten
1 tablespoon baking powder
1 tablespoon chopped shallot
1 teaspoon garlic salt
1 cup milk
2 1/2 cups all-purpose flour
2 tablespoons Gouda cheese, grated
2 tablespoons fresh thyme leaves
1 teaspoon ground cumin seed

1. Preheat the oven to 400°F. Whisk together the butter, milk and egg. In a separate bowl, sift the flour and baking powder. Add the Gouda, shallot, thyme leaves, garlic salt and cumin. With a wooden spoon, stir the dry ingredients into the wet ingredients. Pour the batter into 2 greased loaf pans. Bake the loaves for 50-60 minutes or until an inserted toothpick comes out clean. Cool the loaves on a grill.

2. Preheat the broiler. Cut the loaves into 1/4-inch thick slices. Lightly toast the slices under the broiler.

Oregano Mustard

1/2 cup Dijon mustard
3 tablespoons fresh oregano leaves, finely chopped
2 tablespoons honey
1 garlic clove, finely chopped

1. Whisk all of the ingredients together. Allow the mixture to stand for 30 minutes before serving.

2. Spread 1 teaspoon of mustard onto a slice of Gouda-thyme bread. Top the mustard with a generous slice of pâté. Repeat this process with the remaining pâté.

Oregano Sausage with Tomatoes and Olive Tapenade on Cheese Biscuits

Makes 35 Canapés

Cheese Biscuits

1 cup all-purpose flour
1/2 teaspoon granulated sugar
1/4 cup sweet butter, cold and finely chopped
3/4 cup milk

1 teaspoon baking powder
1/4 teaspoon cream of tartar
1/2 teaspoon salt
1/4 cup cheddar cheese, grated

1. Sift into a bowl the flour, baking powder, sugar, cream of tartar and salt. Add the butter pieces to the dry ingredients. Rub the ingredients between one's hands or pulse the ingredients in a food processor until they resemble a coarse meal. Form the mixture into a fountain and add the milk and cheese to the middle. Gradually combine the wet and dry ingredients, until a wet dough forms. On a floured surface, roll the dough 1/2-inch thick. Fold the dough so it is halved in length and doubled in thickness. Repeat this process 9 times for a flaky, well layered biscuit.

2. Preheat the oven to 375°F. Roll out the dough 1/4-inch thick. With a circular cutter, cut rounds out of the dough and place them on a parchment paper lined baking sheet. Bake the biscuits for 10 minutes or until they are golden brown. Remove them from the oven and cool them on a grill. Slice the biscuits in half.

Tomato Concassé

3 very ripe tomatoes
2 garlic cloves, chopped

1 tablespoon olive oil
3 sprigs fresh thyme

1. With a paring knife, core the tomatoes and mark their bottoms with X's. Plunge the tomatoes into boiling water for 1 minute or until their skins begin to come off. Transfer the tomatoes to a bowl of ice water. When the tomatoes are completely cool, peel their skins. Lay the tomato skins flat on paper towels to dry. Cut the tomatoes in half and remove the seeds.

2. Coarsely chop the tomatoes and place them in a pan with the olive oil, garlic and thyme sprigs. Cover the pan and place it over a low heat. Cook the tomatoes for 10-15 minutes or until they are mush. Cooking time will vary with the ripeness of the tomatoes. At the end of the cooking process, remove the thyme sprigs.

Olive Tapenade

2 cups pitted Kalamata olives
2 tablespoons extra-virgin olive oil
3 garlic cloves

Place the olives and garlic in a blender. While the machine is running, gradually add the olive oil. Purée the olives until the mixture is smooth.

Fried Tomato Skins

Skins of 3 tomatoes
1/2 cup canola oil

Place the oil in a shallow pan. Place the pan over a medium-high heat. When the oil is hot, add the tomato skins. Fry them for 15 seconds on each side. Dry the skins on paper towels.

Oregano Sausage

1/2 cup milk
2 shallots
1 tablespoon ground oregano
3/4 pound pork loin
1/2 cup fresh oregano leaves, chopped
1/2 cup breadcrumbs
1 tablespoon olive oil
3 garlic cloves, chopped
1/4 pound pork fat
2 tablespoons salt

1. Place the meat grinder or food processor bowl in the freezer for 30 minutes prior to use. Combine the milk and breadcrumbs and set them aside. Finely chop the shallots. Place shallots in a shallow pan with the olive oil. Sauté the shallots over a medium heat for 1 minute. Add the ground oregano and garlic to the shallots. Cool the ingredients completely.

2. Alternating between meat and fat, grind the loin and the pork fat through a large-holed plate. Add the fresh oregano, salt and shallots to the meat and regrind it through a small-holed plate. If you do not have access to a meat grinder, place the meat, fat, oregano, salt and cooked shallots in a food processor. Purée the ingredients until they are smooth.

3. Preheat the oven to 350°F. Add the breadcrumb and milk mixture to the meat. Form the forcemeat into small patties and chill them for 30 minutes.

4. Place the patties on a baking sheet with a grill. Roast the patties for 10 minutes or until they are cooked through.

5. Place 1 teaspoon of tapenade on a biscuit half and top with a sausage patty. Top the sausage with 1 teaspoon of tomato concassé. Top the canapé with a fried tomato skin. Repeat this process with the remaining patties. Serve the canapés while the sausage patties are still warm.

Game

    Upon visiting the outback of Australia, I learned about its large population of wild camels. Sitting in the back of a pick-up truck, I witnessed a herd of 100 camels racing across the dry clay of the desert. "When we're not riding them in races, we're eating them." professed our guide.

    Intrigued by the idea of a camel steak, I went to the only eatery for a one-hundred mile radius. Posters on the wall advertised camel meat, claiming it to be leaner and healthier than beef or pork. I ordered the specialty of the house, a camel burger. I found the camel meat to be more flavorful than the burgers we get in the states and the texture was firmer. I have yet to see another menu that includes camel but I recommend it to any advantageous gourmand.

Quail Tamales with Tomato and Avocado Salsa

Makes 20 Canapés

Quail Tamales

3 1/2 pound quails
salt and pepper
1 small yellow onion, finely chopped
1 red pepper, cored, seeded and finely chopped
1 teaspoon dark chili powder
2 tablespoons fresh cilantro leaves, finely chopped
2 cups masa harina
1 teaspoon baking powder
30 dried corn husks

2 tablespoons corn oil
3 tomatoes
1 jalapeño, cored, seeded and finely chopped
1 teaspoon ground cumin seed
2 garlic cloves, finely chopped
1/2 cup lard
1/2 cup chicken broth or water
1 tablespoon salt

1. Preheat the oven to 375°F. Lightly salt and pepper the quails and place them in a roasting pan. Drizzle 1 tablespoon of corn oil over the quails and place them in the oven for 10 minutes or until the meat is medium rare. The meat will continue to cook in the tamales. Cool the quails. Remove the quail meat from the bones and shred it.

2. Core the tomatoes. With a paring knife, mark the bottom of each tomato with an X. Plunge the tomatoes in a pot of boiling water for 1 minute or until the skins begin to come off. Transfer the tomatoes to a bowl of ice water. When the tomatoes have cooled completely peel the skins. Remove any seeds from the tomatoes. Coarsely chop the tomatoes and set them aside.

3. In a deep pan, place the remaining oil over a medium-high heat. When the oil is hot, add the onion, jalapeño, red pepper, cumin, chili powder and garlic. Sauté the vegetables until they are soft, about 10 minutes. Add the tomatoes to the pan. Sauté the ingredients until the tomatoes begin to break apart, about 10 minutes. Transfer the ingredients to a mixing bowl and add the quail meat and cilantro.

4. Rub the lard and 1 cup of the masa harina between your hands or pulse them in a food processor until they form a coarse meal. Whisk the chicken broth, baking powder and salt into the lard and masa harina. Gradually add the remaining masa harina until a loose dough forms.

5. Lay a corn husk flat, with the smooth side facing up. Evenly layer 1 1/2 -2 tablespoons of the masa harina mixture in the center of the husk. Place 1 tablespoon of the quail mixture in the center of the masa harina mixture. Fold the longer edges of the husk towards the center. Then fold the 2 shorter edges toward the center, as one would fold a wallet. Repeat this process with the remaining ingredients.

6. Line the bottom of a steamer with empty corn husks. Top the empty husks with the filled husks. Top the filled husks with more empty husks and tightly seal the steamer. Steam the tamales for 15 minutes or until the dough is cooked through.

Tomato Avocado Salsa

2 tomatoes
1/4 cup fresh cilantro leaves, finely chopped
1 avocado, peeled, seeded and finely chopped
1/2 red onion, finely chopped
2 tablespoons lime juice
1/2 teaspoon salt
1 teaspoon black pepper

1. Remove any seeds from the tomatoes and finely chop them. Combine the tomatoes, cilantro, avocado, red onion, lime juice, salt and pepper. Serve the salsa along side the warm tamales.

Fried Quail Legs with Spicy Lemon Grass Sauce

Makes 24 Legs

Fried Quail Legs

3 tablespoons balsamic vinegar
2 garlic cloves
4 cilantro sprigs, chopped
1/4 cup olive oil
3 cups flour
1 cup cornmeal
1 teaspoon ground ginger
1 teaspoon dark chili powder
1/2 teaspoon white pepper

1 tablespoon dark brown sugar
1 shallot, chopped
1 tablespoon prepared mustard
24 quail legs
2 eggs, beaten
1 teaspoon ground turmeric
1 teaspoon garlic salt
1/2 teaspoon cayenne pepper
3 cups canola oil

1. Whisk together the vinegar, brown sugar, garlic, shallot, cilantro sprigs and mustard. Gradually whisk in the olive oil. Pour this mixture over the quail legs and refrigerate them overnight.

2. Strain the quail legs and discard the marinade. Combine 1 cup of the flour with the cornmeal, turmeric, ginger, garlic salt, chili powder, cayenne pepper and white pepper. Working in batches, dredge the legs in the remaining flour. Then cover the legs with the beaten eggs. After wiping off any excess egg, dredge the legs in the flour and cornmeal mixture.

3. Place the oil in a small pot over a medium-high heat. When the oil reaches 350°F, add a few of the quail legs. Fry each quail leg for 5 minutes, or until it is cooked through. Transfer the legs to paper towels to remove any excess grease. Repeat this process with the remaining quail legs.

Spicy Lemon Grass Sauce

2 tomatoes
1 tablespoon olive oil
1 teaspoon ground turmeric
1 dried chili
2 garlic cloves, chopped
1/4 cup chopped fresh basil

1 lemon grass stalk
1 tablespoon fresh ginger, peeled and chopped
1/4 teaspoon ground cardamom
2 shallots, chopped
1 cup water
1 1/2 cups mayonnaise

1. Core the tomatoes. With a paring knife, mark the bottom of each tomato with an X. Plunge the tomatoes in a pot of boiling water for 1 minute or until their skins begin to come off. Transfer the tomatoes to a bowl of ice water. When the tomatoes have cooled completely, the skins should peel off easily. Remove the skins and any seeds from the tomatoes and coarsely chop them.

2. Lay the lemon grass stalk on a cutting board. Cut off the root and discard it. With the smooth side of a mallet or a small pot, pound the white part of the lemongrass until it breaks apart. Finely chop the white part and discard the tough, green stalk.

3. In a shallow pan over a medium-high heat, place the olive oil. When the oil is hot add the tomatoes and lemon grass. Reduce the heat to medium-low and add the ginger, turmeric, cardamom, dried chili, shallots, garlic and water. Lightly simmer the mixture for 20 minutes or until the tomatoes break apart. Add the basil. Transfer the mixture to a blender or food processor. Purée the mixture until it is smooth. Strain the mixture through a fine sieve and cool the juice. Whisk in the mayonnaise. Serve the quail legs warm with the dipping sauce on the side.

Roasted Quail with Avocado and Tomato Cream on Tomatillo Tortilla Chips

Makes 40 Canapés

Roasted Quail

2 green onions, finely chopped
1 garlic clove, minced
1 teaspoon chili powder
2 tablespoons apple cider vinegar
8 quails

5 cilantro sprigs, finely chopped
1 teaspoon ground cumin seed
2 tablespoons lime juice
1/4 cup olive oil

1. In a mixing bowl, whisk together the green onions, cilantro, garlic, cumin, chili powder, lime juice and vinegar. Gradually whisk in the olive oil. Pour the mixture over the quails and marinate them overnight.

2. Preheat the oven to 350°F. Strain the quails and discard the marinade. Place the quails in a roasting pan. Roast the quails for 15-20 minutes or until the meat is cooked through. Cool the quails.

3. Debone the quail meat and slice it into thin strips. Set the quail meat aside.

Avocado and Tomato Cream

1 avocado, peeled, seeded and chopped
1 teaspoon garlic salt
3 tablespoons lime juice
2 small tomatoes

1 jalapeño, cored, seeded and chopped
1 teaspoon black pepper
1 cup sour cream

1. In a blender or food processor, place the avocado, jalapeño, garlic salt, pepper and lime juice. Purée the ingredients until they are smooth. Whisk the purée into the sour cream.

2. Core the tomatoes. With a paring knife, mark the bottom of each tomato with an X. Plunge the tomatoes in a pot of boiling water for 1 minute or until their skin begins to come off. Transfer the tomatoes to a bowl of ice water. When the tomatoes have cooled completely, the skin should peel off easily. Remove any seeds from the tomatoes and finely chop them. Add the tomatoes to the sour cream mixture. Chill the cream.

Tomatillo Chips

5 tomatillos, husks and cores removed and coarsely chopped
1 shallot, chopped
2 garlic cloves, minced
1 teaspoon ground coriander
1 teaspoon ground ginger
2 cups water
1 1/2 cups all purpose flour
1/2 teaspoon salt
2 cups canola oil
2 cups red leaf lettuce leaves
2 1/2 tablespoons cold lard or vegetable shortening, chopped into small pieces

1. In a pot over a medium heat, place the tomatillos, shallot, garlic, coriander, ginger and water. Simmer the ingredients for 45 minutes or until the tomatillos break apart. Strain the ingredients through a fine sieve and reserve the juice. Add enough water to the juice to produce 5 tablespoons of liquid.

2. In a mixing bowl, combine the flour, salt and lard. Rub this mixture between one's hands or pulse it in a food processor, until it resembles a coarse meal. With a wooden spoon, stir in the tomatillo juice and enough water to produce a firm but sticky dough. Divide the dough into 10 portions. Allow the portions to rest for 30 minutes.

3. On a lightly floured surface, roll out each portion into a paper-thin disk. Over a high heat, place a skillet. When the skillet is hot, add a disk and heat it until it puffs up. Flip the disk and heat the other side until it is slightly brown. Repeat this process with the remaining disks.

4. Cut the disks into triangles. Place the oil in a pot over a medium-high heat. When the oil reaches 375°F, add a few triangles. Fry the triangles for 1-2 minutes or until they are golden. Transfer the triangles to paper towels to remove any excess grease. Repeat this process with the remaining triangles.

5. Tear the lettuce leaves into bite-size pieces. Place a piece of lettuce on a tomatillo chip. Top the chip with 1 teaspoon of the avocado and tomato sour cream. Place a few strips of the quail on top. Repeat this process with the remaining quail meat. Serve the canapés with the quail meat warm or chilled.

Smoked Pheasant with Hummus on Parmesan Biscuits

Makes 45 Canapés

Smoked Pheasant

2 cups water
2 tablespoons brandy
1 thyme sprig
4 juniper berries, slightly crushed
4 1/2 pound pheasant breasts, boneless

2 tablespoons salt
1 tablespoon honey
1 bay leaf
1 teaspoon dried oregano leaves
maple wood chips

1. In a pot over a high heat, place the water, salt, brandy, honey, thyme, bay leaf, juniper berries and oregano. Bring the brine to a boil. Cool the brine completely.

2. Add the pheasants to the cold brine. Refrigerate the pheasants overnight.

3. Prepare the hot smoker with maple wood chips. Strain the pheasants and discard the brine. Smoke the pheasants for 10 minutes. Place the pheasants in a 375°F oven for 10 minutes or until they have cooked through. Cool the breasts. Cutting across the grain of the flesh, thinly slice the pheasant.

Parmesan Biscuits

2 cups all-purpose flour
2 teaspoons light brown sugar
1/4 cup chives, chopped
6 ounces Parmesan cheese

1 teaspoon baking powder
1/2 teaspoon cream of tartar
1/2 cup cold butter, cut into small pieces
1 cup milk

1. In a food processor bowl, combine the flour, baking powder, brown sugar, cream of tartar, garlic powder and cumin. Add the pieces of lard and pulse until the mixture resembles a coarse meal. Transfer the mixture to a large bowl and add the Parmesan. Gradually stir in the milk until a firm dough forms. Refrigerate the dough for 30 minutes.

2. Preheat the oven to 400°F. On a floured surface, roll out the dough to 1/2-inch thick rectangle. Fold one-half of the dough over the other half, making the dough half its original length but double its original thickness. Again, roll the dough out to 1/2-inch thick. Repeat this process 9 more times for a flaky dough. Roll the dough 1/2-inch thick. Dust a small round cutter with flour. Cut small rounds out the dough. Place the rounds on a well-greased baking sheet. Bake the biscuits for 10 minutes or until they are lightly brown. Cool the biscuits on a grill. Halve the biscuits.

Hummus

2 cups cooked chic peas, rinsed if canned
2 garlic cloves, chopped
1 tablespoon tahini
2 tablespoons lemon juice
1 teaspoon salt
3 tablespoons extra virgin olive oil
1 Radicchio head, cored and chopped

1. Place in a blender or food processor, the chic peas, garlic, tahini, lemon juice and salt. Blend the ingredients until they are smooth. While the machine is running, slowly add the olive oil.

2. Place 1 tablespoon of hummus on a biscuit half. Top the hummus with some radicchio and then a few pheasant slices. Repeat this process with the remaining pheasant slices. Serve the biscuits with the pheasant meat warm or chilled.

Sliced Rabbit with Carrot Relish on Rye Toasts

Makes 30 Canapés

Rye Toasts

1 tablespoon dry active yeast
3/4 cup warm water, 105-115°F
1 tablespoon dark brown sugar
1 tablespoon cumin seeds
1/2 cup rye flour
1 teaspoon garlic salt

1 teaspoon granulated sugar
2 tablespoons molasses
1 tablespoon fennel seeds
1 tablespoon unsalted butter, softened
1 1/2 cups all purpose flour
cornmeal

1. Sprinkle the yeast and sugar over 1/4 cup of the warm water. Place the mixture in a warm, draft-free area for 10 minutes, or until it is foamy.

2. Add the molasses, brown sugar, fennel seeds, cumin seeds and the remaining water to the yeast mixture. Stir the ingredients until they are completely incorporated. Add the softened butter and rye flour. In a separate bowl, combine the flour and garlic salt. Gradually add the flour mixture to the yeast mixture. Mix until the dough comes together. On a floured surface, knead the dough until it is smooth and elastic, about 10 minutes. Place the dough in an oiled bowl and flip it to oil all sides. Cover the dough and place it in a warm area. Allow the dough to rise until it has doubled in bulk.

3. Preheat the oven to 375°F. Generously sprinkle cornmeal onto a baking sheet. Gently deflate the dough and form it into a loaf. Place the loaf, seam side down, on the baking sheet. Cover the loaf and place it in a warm area. Allow the loaf to rise until it has doubled in bulk.

4. Bake the loaf for 30-35 minutes, or until a tap on its bottom sounds hollow. Cool the loaf on a grill.

5. Preheat the broiler. Cut the loaf into 1/2-inch thick slices. Place the slices under the broiler until they are well-toasted.

Sliced Rabbit

2 tablespoons rice wine vinegar
1/2 teaspoon ground allspice
2 thyme sprigs
salt and pepper

2 garlic cloves, finely chopped
1/4 cup olive oil
4 rabbit legs, deboned

1. Whisk together the vinegar, garlic, allspice and 3 tablespoons of the olive oil. Add the thyme sprigs and pour the mixture over the rabbit. Allow the rabbit to marinate for at least 2 hours.

2. Preheat the oven to 375°F. Strain the rabbit and discard the marinade. Place the remaining olive oil in a shallow pan over a medium-high heat. When the oil is hot, place the rabbit in the pan. Brown the rabbit on all sides. Place the rabbit in the oven for 10 minutes or until it is cooked through. Take the rabbit out of the oven and allow it to rest for 5 minutes. Cutting across the grain of the flesh, thinly slice the rabbit.

Carrot-Sage Relish

3 carrots, peeled and finely chopped
1 tablespoon unsalted butter
1 teaspoon salt
1/2 small red onion, finely chopped
1 tablespoon extra virgin olive oil

1 cup water
1 teaspoon granulated sugar
1/2 teaspoon ginger powder
1/4 cup fresh sage leaves, finely chopped
1 teaspoon freshly ground black pepper

1. In a deep pan, place the carrots, water, butter, sugar, salt and ginger powder. Place the pan over a medium heat. Partially cover the pan and simmer the carrots until all of the water has evaporated. Cool the carrots completely.

2. Combine the carrots, red onion, sage leaves, olive oil and black pepper.

3. Place 1 teaspoon of carrot relish on a rye toast. Top the relish with a few rabbit slices. Serve the canapés while the rabbit is still warm.

Rabbit, Tarragon and Sunflower Seed Terrine with Glazed Parsnips on Dill Toasts

Makes 45 Canapés

Dill Toasts

1 tablespoon dry active yeast
1 1/4 cups warm water, 105-115°F
1/4 cup fresh dill, finely chopped
2 tablespoons honey
1 cup rye flour
Cornmeal

1 teaspoon light brown sugar
1 egg, beaten
2 tablespoons unsalted butter, melted
2 cups all-purpose flour
1 teaspoon salt

1. Sprinkle the yeast and brown sugar over 1/4 cup of the warm water. Allow the yeast to rise in a warm, draft free area until it is foamy, about 10 minutes.

2. Add the egg, dill, butter, honey and the remaining warm water to the yeast mixture. Whisk the ingredients until they are completely incorporated. In a separate bowl, combine the flours and salt. Gradually add the flour mixture to the yeast mixture, until a firm dough forms. On a floured surface, knead the dough until it is smooth and elastic, about 10 minutes. Place the dough in an oiled bowl and flip it to oil all sides. Cover the bowl and place it in a warm area. Allow the dough to rise until it has doubled in bulk.

3. Preheat the oven to 350°F. Generously sprinkle cornmeal onto a baking sheet. Gently deflate the dough and divide it into 2 loaves. Stretch one of the halves into a rectangle. Beginning at one of the wider edges, roll the dough into a long, cylindrical loaf. Repeat with the other half. Place the loaves, seam sides down, on the baking sheet. Cover the loaves and allow them to rise, in a warm area until they have doubled in bulk.

4. Bake the loaves for 45 minutes. Cool the loaves on a grill.

5. Preheat the broiler. Cut the loaves into 1/2-inch thick slices. Place the slices close to the broiler until they are well toasted.

Rabbit, Tarragon and Sunflower Terrine

20 slices center cut bacon
7 ounces pork butt, cubed
2 tablespoons port wine
1 teaspoon salt
3/4 cup heavy cream, very cold
14 ounces cleaned rabbit meat, cubed
2 shallots, finely chopped
2 eggs, slightly beaten
1/2 teaspoon white pepper
1 tablespoon prepared mustard
2 tablespoons fresh tarragon leaves, finely chopped
3 tablespoons sunflower seeds, unsalted
Boiling water

1. Place the bacon slices in a pot. Fill the pot with enough cold water to cover the bacon. Place the pot over a high heat. Bring the bacon to a boil and reduce the heat to medium-high. Removing any scum from the surface, simmer the bacon for 20 minutes. Strain the bacon and cool it completely. Dry the bacon on paper towels.

2. Generously butter a terrine mold. Line the mold with overlapping bacon slices and chill it.

3. Preheat the oven to 225°F. Place the rabbit meat, pork butt and shallot in a food processor. Purée the meat until it is smooth. With the machine running add the port, eggs, salt, pepper, cream, mustard and tarragon. Fold the sunflower seeds into the mixture. Pour the mixture into the bacon-lined terrine mold and layer the bacon slices over the top. Line a roasting pan with 2 layers of paper towels. Place the terrine mold in the center of the roasting pan. Fill the roasting pan with enough boiling water to reach 2/3rds the height of the terrine. Place the roasting pan in the oven for 1 hour and 45 minutes. Chill the terrine in its mold for at least 6 hours.

4. Turn the mold over onto a flat surface. Cut the terrine into 1/2-inch thick slices.

Glazed Parsnips

4 large parsnips
1 teaspoon salt
3/4 cup chicken stock or water
1 tablespoon unsalted butter
1 tablespoon dark brown sugar

1. Preheat the oven to 350°F. Wash and peel the parsnips. Thinly slice the parsnips. Place the parsnips, butter, salt, brown sugar and chicken stock in a roasting pan. Place the roasting pan in the oven for 30 minutes or until the parsnips are tender.

2. Place a slice of terrine on a dill toast. Top the terrine with one or two parsnip slices and serve.

Rabbit Sausage with Garlic Roasted Shallots on Oregano Focaccia

Makes 20 Canapés

Rabbit Sausage

- 1 3 pound whole rabbit
- 3 garlic cloves, chopped
- 1/2 cup apple cider vinegar
- 2 tablespoons light brown sugar
- 2 tablespoons olive oil
- 1/2 stalk celery, coarsely chopped
- 1/2 cup dry white wine
- 2 tablespoons milk
- 1 pound pork fat cut into small cubes
- 1 teaspoon Chinese Five Spice
- 4 tablespoons Dijon mustard
- 1/2 cup flat leaf parsley leaves, chopped
- 1 teaspoon freshly ground black pepper
- 1 teaspoon ground allspice
- 2 shallots, coarsely chopped
- 1 small carrot, peeled and chopped
- 1 bay leaf
- 2 tablespoons breadcrumbs
- 1 tablespoon salt

1. Set the rib cage of the rabbit aside. Debone the rest of the rabbit meat. Discard the fat and reserve all the bones and nerves. Cut the rabbit flesh into cubes. In a bowl whisk together the Dijon, 2 of the garlic cloves, 1/4 cup of the parsley, cider vinegar, black pepper, brown sugar and the allspice. Place the rabbit flesh and rib cage in the marinade and refrigerate it overnight.

2. Sauce: Coarsely chop the rabbit bones. Place the bones, with 1 tablespoon of the olive oil, in a pot over a medium-high heat. Stir the bones only once or twice; the proteins in the bones will stick to the bottom of the pot and give the sauce a full flavor. When the bones are brown, add the shallots, celery and carrot. Sauté the vegetables until they are tender, about 10 minutes. Increase the heat to high and add the white wine. Boil the wine for 2-3 minutes. Add cold water to the height of the bones. With a wooden spoon, scrape the brown bits off of the bottom of the pot. Add the remaining garlic, bay leaf and rabbit nerves to the pot and simmer the liquid over a medium heat for 2 hours. Strain the sauce and reduce the liquid by half.

3. Sausage: Place the grinder attachment or food processor bowl in the freezer for 30 minutes prior to use. In a bowl, combine the milk and breadcrumbs. Strain the rabbit flesh and discard the marinade. Alternating the rabbit meat and the pork fat, grind the flesh through a large-holed plate. Add the salt, five spice and 1/4 cup of parsley to the forcemeat. Regrind the meat through a fine-holed plate. If using a food processor, purée the meat, fat, salt, five spice, oregano, parsley and allspice until smooth. Incorporate the breadcrumbs and milk with the meat. Refrigerate the forcemeat.

4. Preheat the oven to 375°F. Form the forcemeat into small patties and place them on a greased baking sheet. Roast the patties for 5 minutes on each side or until cooked through.

5. Rabbit meat: Over a medium-high heat, place a pan with the remaining olive oil. Remove the rib cage from the marinade and lightly salt and pepper it. Place the rib cage in the hot oil. Brown the rib cage for 5 minutes on each side. Place the rib cage in the oven for 20 minutes or until the meat is cooked through. Remove the rib cage and let it rest for 5 minutes. Remove the flaps of skin from the rib cage. Cut the flesh from both sides of the rib cage. An average rib cage yields 2 1/4-inch thick slices on each side. Cut the slices into thin strips and toss the strips in the sauce.

Focaccia

1 tablespoon dry active yeast
1 cup warm water, 105-115°F
1 tablespoon salt
2 tablespoons olive oil

1 teaspoon granulated sugar
3 1/2 cups bread flour
1/4 cup fresh basil, chopped
Kosher salt

1. Dissolve the yeast and sugar in the warm water. Let the yeast rise in a warm place, for 10 minutes or until it is foamy.

2. In a separate bowl, combine the flour, salt and basil. Form these dry ingredients into a well. Place in the center of the well the yeast mixture, and olive oil. Gradually combine the wet and dry ingredients until a shaggy dough has formed. On a lightly floured surface, knead the dough for 15 minutes or until it is smooth and elastic.

3. Place the dough in an oiled bowl and flip it to oil all sides. Cover the dough and place it in a warm, draft free area, until it has doubled in bulk.

4. Preheat the oven to 425ºF. On a floured surface, gently deflate the dough and knead it for 15 minutes, or until it is smooth and elastic. Roll the dough 1/2-inch thick and place it on a floured baking sheet. Cover the dough and let it rise until it has doubled in size.

5. Press into the dough with one's fingers, forming a grid of dents, about 1/2-inch away from each other. Sprinkle the dough with kosher salt and bake it for 15-20 minutes. Cool the focaccia on a grill.

6. When the focaccia is cool, slice it into squares.

Garlic Roasted Shallots

5 shallots
1 tablespoon olive oil
2 garlic cloves, finely chopped

1. Preheat the oven to 400ºF. Place the unpeeled shallots in a roasting pan. Drizzle the shallots with the olive oil and place them in the oven. Roast the shallots for 20 minutes. Remove the shallots from the oven and cool them.

2. Remove the roots and skins from the shallots. Slice the shallots into thin strips. Mix the shallots with the garlic.

3. Preheat the oven to 400ºF. Spread 1 tablespoon of the shallots on a focaccia slice. Top it with a sausage patty. Top the sausage patty with a slice of rabbit meat. Place the canapés in the oven for 3-4 minutes to warm. Serve the canapés warm.

Buffalo Patties with Radicchio Sauce on Cilantro Pita Chips

Makes 40 Canapés

Cilantro Pita Chips

1 teaspoon dry active yeast
3/4 cup warm water, 105-115°F
1 tablespoon honey
2 cups bread flour

1 tablespoon olive oil
2 tablespoons fresh cilantro leaves, finely chopped
2 tablespoons fresh parsley leaves, finely chopped
1 teaspoon garlic salt

1. In a mixing bowl, combine the yeast, olive oil, warm water, cilantro, parsley and honey. In a separate bowl, incorporate the flour and garlic salt. Gradually add the flour to the yeast mixture, until a firm dough forms. On a floured surface, knead the dough until it is smooth and elastic, about 10 minutes. Place the dough in an oiled bowl and flip it to oil all sides. Cover the bowl with a towel and place it in a warm place. Allow the dough to rise until it has doubled in bulk.

2. Gently deflate the dough and divide it into 5 portions. Preheat the oven to 500°F. Working with one's palm on a floured surface, form each portion of dough into a 1/4-inch thick round. Let the portions rest for 10 minutes. Heat a baking sheet in the oven. Place the rounds on the baking sheet and bake them until they puff up and brown, about 3 minutes on each side.

3. Preheat the broiler. Peel apart the pitas to form 2 rounds from each pita. Cut the rounds into triangles. Place the triangles under the broiler and toast them until golden-brown.

Radicchio Sauce

2 heads of raddichio
3 cups boiling water
1 garlic clove, minced
1/4 cup lemon juice

1 tablespoon red wine vinegar
1 tablespoon tahini
1/2 teaspoon salt
3 tablespoons sour cream

1. Core the Radicchio and remove any tough spines from the leaves. Chop the Radicchio and place it in a mixing bowl. Pour the vinegar over the Radicchio and toss it to coat. Pour the boiling water into the mixing bowl. Allow the Radicchio to stand in the water for 5 minutes. Strain the Radicchio and plunge it in cold water to cool it completely. Strain the Radicchio and pat it dry.

2. In a blender, place the tahini, garlic, salt, lemon juice, sour cream and 1 tablespoon of water. Blend the ingredients until they are smooth. Add the Radicchio and chill the sauce.

Buffalo Patties

2 cups walnuts, chopped
2 pounds ground buffalo meat
1 tablespoon salt
1/2 teaspoon ground allspice
3 tablespoons yogurt
3 tablespoons olive oil
1 stalk fresh lemon grass
1 garlic clove, minced
1 teaspoon black pepper
2 scallions, finely chopped
1/2 cup breadcrumbs

1. Preheat the oven to 450°F. Place the walnuts in a roasting pan. Place the pan in the oven. Roast the nuts for 5-8 minutes or until they are aromatic.

2. Lay the lemon grass stalk on a cutting board. Cut off the root and discard it. With the smooth side of a mallet or a small pot, pound the white part of the lemon grass until it breaks apart. Finely chop the white part and discard the tough, green stalk.

3. In a mixing bowl, place the walnuts, lemon grass, buffalo meat, garlic, allspice, scallions, yogurt and breadcrumbs. Incorporate the ingredients thoroughly and chill the mixture for 30 minutes.

5. Form a small patty out of 2 tablespoons of the buffalo mixture. Repeat this process with the remaining buffalo mixture. Refrigerate the patties for 30 minutes.

6. Place 1 tablespoon of the olive oil in a shallow pan over a medium-high heat. Working in batches, add the patties to the pan and brown them for 5 minutes on each side or until they are cooked through. Remove any excess grease by transferring the patties to paper towels. Cook the remaining patties in the same fashion.

7. Place 1 tablespoon of the Radicchio sauce on a pita chip. Top the sauce with a warm buffalo patty. Repeat this process with the remaining patties. Serve while the buffalo is still warm.

Cajun Smoked Duck Breast with Fennel on Tangy Chive Toasts

Makes 30 Canapés

Cajun Smoked Duck Breast

2 duck breasts, boneless
1 teaspoon ground mace
1 teaspoon ground allspice
1 teaspoon dried thyme
1 teaspoon black pepper
1 teaspoon chili powder
1 tablespoon onion flakes
Maple wood chips

1 bay leaf, crumbled
1 teaspoon ground cloves
2 teaspoons cayenne pepper
1 teaspoon garlic powder
1 teaspoon lemon pepper
1 tablespoon paprika
2 tablespoons kosher salt

1. Combine the bay leaf, mace, cloves, allspice, cayenne, thyme, garlic powder, black pepper, lemon pepper, chili powder, paprika, onion flakes and kosher salt. Press the flesh of the breasts into the spice mixture. Place the breasts in a colander over a drainage bowl and refrigerate them for 2 days. Flip the breasts and drain the liquid from the drainage bowl after 24 hours.

2. Prepare the smoker with maple wood chips. Hot smoke the breasts for 10 minutes. Place the breasts in a 400°F oven for 5 minutes, depending on thickness of the breasts to finish the cooking process. Allow the meat to rest for 5 minutes. Cutting across the grain of flesh, thinly slice the breasts. Set the duck slices aside.

Tangy Chive Bread

2 cups all-purpose flour
1 teaspoon salt
3/4 cup Parmesan cheese, grated
1/4 cup water
1/4 cup sweet butter, melted
1/4 cup chives, finely chopped

3 teaspoons baking powder
3/4 cup Pepper Jack cheese, grated
1/2 cup whipping cream
1 tablespoon prepared mustard
2 eggs, beaten
1 tablespoon black pepper

1. Preheat the oven to 350°F. In a bowl, combine the flour, baking powder, salt and both the grated cheeses. In a separate bowl, whisk together the cream, water, mustard, butter, eggs, chives and pepper. Incorporate the 2 mixtures. Pour the batter into a well-greased loaf pan and bake the bread for 60 minutes, or until an inserted toothpick comes out clean. Cool the loaf on a grill.

2. Preheat the broiler. Cut the loaf into 1/2-inch thick slices. Place the slices near the broiler. Toast the slices to a light brown.

Julienne of Fennel

1 large head of fennel
3 tablespoons lemon juice
1/4 cup fresh dill, finely chopped

Remove the stalks and tough outer leaves from the fennel. Core the fennel and slice the leaves into thin strips. Place the strips in a mixing bowl. Add the lemon juice and dill to the strips.
Place a spoonful of fennel strips on a tangy chive toast. Top the fennel with a slice of duck breast. Repeat this process with the remaining slices of duck breast. Serve warm or chilled.

Duck Sausage Rolls with Sweet Mustard Sauce

Makes 40 Canapés

Duck Sausage

1/2 pound pork fat
2 tablespoons soy sauce
1/4 cup breadcrumbs
2 shallots
4 garlic cloves, chopped
1/4 cup fresh parsley leaves, finely chopped

2 pounds duck meat
4 tablespoons raspberry vinegar
1/4 cup milk
1 tablespoon olive oil
1/4 cup fresh sage leaves, finely chopped
1 tablespoon salt

1. Cut the fat into cubes and chill them. Cube the duck meat and place it in a mixing bowl. In a separate bowl, whisk together the soy sauce and vinegar. Add the soy sauce and vinegar to the duck meat and chill it for 4 hours.

2. Place the meat grinder attachment or food processor bowl into the freezer, for 30 minutes prior to use. In a separate bowl, combine the milk and breadcrumbs and set them aside.

3. Finely chop the shallots. In a pan over a medium-high heat, sauté the shallots in the olive oil. When the shallots are translucent, add the chopped garlic and cook them for 1 minute. Transfer the shallots and garlic to a bowl and chill them.

4. Drain the marinade from the duck meat. Add the cooled shallots, sage, parsley and salt to the duck meat. Assemble the grinder with a large-holed plate. Grind the cubes of fat and duck meat, alternating between the two. Insert a small-holed plate into the grinder. Regrind the meat and fat. If using a food processor, purée the meat and fat until they are smooth. Add the shallots, garlic, breadcrumbs and milk and chill the forcemeat.

Pizza Dough

1 1/2 cups all purpose flour, sifted
1 teaspoon dry active yeast
1 tablespoon olive oil

1 teaspoon salt
1/4 cup warm water, 105-115°F

1. In a bowl, combine the flour and salt. Add the yeast to the bowl. Forming a fountain, make a large hole in the dry ingredients. Add the warm water and the oil to the middle of the fountain. Gradually combine the wet and dry ingredients. Add more water if needed. On a lightly floured surface, knead the dough for 10 minutes or until it is smooth and elastic. Place the dough in an oiled bowl and flip it to oil all sides. Cover

the dough with plastic wrap and let it rise in a warm, draft free area for 90 minutes.

2. On a floured surface, gently deflate the dough and knead it for 5 minutes. Split the dough into 10 portions. Chill the dough until ready for stuffing.

Sweet Mustard Sauce

1 cup duck stock or water
3 tablespoons honey
1/2 teaspoon garlic powder

1/2 cup dijion mustard
1 tablespoon blackstrap molasses
1/2 teaspoon ground turmeric

In a pot over a low heat, whisk together the stock, dijion mustard, honey, molasses, garlic powder, curry and turmeric. Keep the sauce warm.

Sausage Rolls: Preheat the oven to 425°F. Roll each potion into an 1/8th-inch thick rectangle. Brush a rectangle of dough with mustard sauce. Leaving 1/2-inch of one of the shorter sides bare, spread 2 tablespoons of sausage in an even layer on the dough. Carefully roll the dough and sausage into a tight cylinder. End with the bare end of the dough. Repeat this process with the remaining dough. Place the rolls on a non-stick baking sheet, seam side down and bake them at 425°F for 20 minutes. Slice the rolls into thirds or quarters.

Mini Pizzas: Preheat the oven to 425°F. Roll each portion of dough into a 1/8th-inch thick circle. Brush dough circles with the mustard sauce. Place 2 tablespoons of sausage on the center of a circle. Repeat this process with the remaining dough. Place the mini pizzas on a non-stick baking sheet and bake them at 425°F for 15-20 minutes.

Mini Calzones: Preheat the oven to 425°F. Roll the portions into 1/8th-inch thick ovals. Brush water around the edge of each oval. Place 2 tablespoons of forcemeat on one side of an oval and top it with 1 tablespoon of sweet mustard sauce. Fold over the other side of the oval; it should form the shape of a clam. Press the edges together for a firm seal. Cut slits in the top of the dough for ventilation. Repeat this process with the remaining dough. Place the calzones on a non-stick baking sheet and bake them at 425°F for 15 minutes.

Serve the canapés warm with a bowl of the remaining sweet mustard sauce for dipping.

Confit of Duck with Spinach and Basil in Phyllo Dough

Makes 30 Canapés

Confit of Duck with Spinach and Basil

4 garlic cloves, minced
1/4 cup granulated sugar
4 duck legs
6 cups spinach leaves
2 shallots, finely chopped
8 ounces goat cheese
3 tablespoons olive oil

1/4 cup kosher salt
3 tablespoons half-cracked black pepper
1 quart clarified duck or goose fat
1 teaspoon + 1 cup unsalted butter
1/4 cup fresh basil leaves, finely chopped
15 sheets of phyllo dough

1. In a bowl, combine half of the garlic with the kosher salt, sugar and the half-cracked black pepper. Press the flesh sides of the duck legs into the spice mixture. Place the legs, flesh side down, in a colander or perforated pan and place a plate on top of them. Weight the plate with a brick or heavy cans. Place the colander over a bowl to catch any liquid. Refrigerate the legs for 48 hours, draining any liquid every 12 hours.

2. Preheat the oven to 200°F. Melt the duck fat over a medium heat. Wipe the spice mixture off of the legs. Place the legs in a deep pot, skin side down and cover them with the melted duck fat. The legs should be completely covered. Cover the pot tightly and place it in the oven. Allow the legs to slowly cook in the fat for about 3-4 hours or until the meat comes off the bone easily. Take the legs out of the fat and cool them. Strain the fat and reserve it for another use. When the legs have cooled completely, remove the meat from them and shred it. Discard the bones and skin and place the meat in a mixing bowl.

3. Remove the stems from the spinach by holding a leaf and twisting the stem off at the base. Swish the spinach leaves in a bowl of cold water until they are free of dirt.

4. In a shallow pan over a medium-high heat, melt one teaspoon of butter. When the butter begins to sizzle, add the chopped shallots and sauté them. When the shallots are translucent, add the remaining garlic and the spinach to the pan. Cover the pan and steam the spinach for 2 minutes or until is has completely wilted. Squeeze any excess water from the spinach and add the leaves to the duck meat.

5. Incorporate the basil, goat cheese, duck meat and spinach. Melt the remaining butter. Place the stack of phyllo sheets on a cutting board. Cut the sheets into 3-inch wide and 6-inch long strips. Place one of the strips onto your work area. Place a slightly damp towel over the remaining sheets. Brush the strip with butter and top with another strip. Butter the second strip and top it with a third. Place about 2 tablespoons of the spinach mixture on a shorter end of the phyllo. Fold the phyllo over the filling to make a triangle. Continue to fold the phyllo as one would a flag. Seal the end with some of the melted butter. Repeat this process with the remaining sheets of phyllo.

6. Place a skillet over a medium-high heat, when the pan is hot add 1 tablespoon of the olive oil. When the oil is hot add a few of the triangles. Brown the triangles on both sides. Work in batches and add more oil as necessary. Serve the triangles warm.

After-anecdote

One of my methods of experimentation in the kitchen is to combine different flavors and textures, using traditional techniques. My experimentation periods for a single technique lasts about a week. Hence, my friends have reaped the benefits from such experiments as soufflé week, sushi roll week and savory cheesecake week.

During pâté week, I instructed all of my friends to buy crackers because they'd soon have generous portions of pâté.

After a rigorous week with various livers, I had exhausted my supply of aluminum foil before I had finished my last pâté. I went to the apartment below mine, which was filled with young men trying to reduce their rent by maximizing their occupancy level. They gave me a strip of foil and I promised to return the favor. The next day I brought them a large plate of pâté and some homemade crackers. "Here's some pâté and crackers, enjoy!" I said. They thanked me and I left.

Two weeks later, I was walking to the store. One of the men from downstairs yelled to me from his porch, "Hey, what's pâté?" Knowing it was still in their refrigerator, I yelled back, "It's like a fancy meat loaf. Throw it away and eat the crackers."

Appetite-Stimulating Ingredients

Allspice

Allspice is the dried berry from an evergreen tree in the myrtle family. Grown mostly in Jamaica, Mexico and Central America, the flavor of this spice resembles that of cinnamon, nutmeg and cloves. The berries of allspice will stay freshest if bought whole and ground as needed. Although a pinch too much can be over powering, allspice is a welcome flavor in deserts and entrées. Allspice is a necessary ingredient in many spice mixes, including Ras al Hanout from Morocco.

Allspice contains potassium, calcium, magnesium and iron. This berry stimulates the appetite and digestion. Allspice alleviates flatulence and rheumatism.

Apricots

The apricot lends its flavor well to savory as well as sweet dishes. Apricots are delicious fruits that become ripe during the summer. When an apricot is ripe its skin becomes smooth.

When purchasing apricots, avoid those with cracks, blemishes or white spots. Choose apricots that are strong scented with a soft, velvety skin.

Wash apricots just before using. Once cut, the flesh of an apricot may become discolored due to oxidization. Rubbing lemon juice on the flesh will prevent browning. One can remove the skin of an apricot by plunging it in boiling water and then transferring it to ice water. After this process the skin peels away easily.

Apricot seeds can be blanched, peeled and eaten. Their flavor resembles that of almonds.

Apricots are rich in potassium. They also contain vitamin C and a high level of vitamin A. The apricot fights anemia and works as an astringent. Apricots stimulate the appetite. The pectin in apricots helps prevent colon cancer.

Avocado

The avocado is the fruit of a tree native to Central and South America. Avocados reach their peak in the spring. The two most popular varieties are the Haas and the Fuerte.

When buying an avocado, choose one that is heavy for its size and free of black spots or bruises. An avocado that is too soft is over ripe. An avocado can finish ripening in a paper bag.

When cutting an avocado, rub it with lemon juice to prevent discoloration. The avocado does not stand up well to cooking. Boiling detracts from the subtle flavor of an avocado.

Avocados benefit the arteries, lower cholesterol levels and dilate blood vessels. Avocados are a rich source of Glutatione, which is a powerful antioxidant that blocks thirty different types of carcinogens and proliferation of AIDS in test tube experiments. An energizing food, the avocado also helps fight cataracts and blocks sperm deterioration. An excellent source of potassium and folic acid, avocados are good for the stomach and intestines. Due to its high zinc content, the avocado improves the sense of smell, thus stimulating the appetite.

Basil

Basil is a wonderful herb that helps to define Italian cuisine. Sweet basil, *Ocimum basilicum*, is the most popular. For a colorful presentation, use purple basil. The pungent dark leaves are excellent with seafood.

When buying basil, choose the brightest, greenest leaves available. The smaller leaves tend to be more tender. Avoid basil with flowers since they are an indication of bitterness.

Store basil in the refrigerator, in a perforated bag with a damp towel. Wash basil just before using. Preserve its color and flavor by adding it to dishes at the very last minute. Basil stems are very potent; use them sparingly to flavor sauces and stocks.

Basil contains potassium, calcium and vitamin C. In addition to stimulating one's appetite, basil aids digestion. This wonderful herb also acts as an antispasmodic, an antiseptic and a tonic. Basil fights migraines and insomnia.

Beets

Beets lend their sweet flavor and vibrant colors to a variety of dishes. Beets are at their best during spring and summer. The first beets of summer taste as sweet as sugar cubes.

Choose beets that are firm, with smooth skins and healthy green leaves. The most flavorful beets have a deep red color and are free of bruises. Large or elongated beets may be fibrous. Although beets will keep in the refrigerator for 2-4 weeks, their leaves last only a few days. Prepare beet leaves as one would spinach.

Avoid piercing the skin of the beet during the cooking process. This will allow the color and nutrients to escape. Lemon juice will remove beet stains from the skin. Wearing rubber gloves while peeling beets, prevents getting stains on one's hands.

Excellent sources of potassium and vitamin A, beets also contain vitamin C, magnesium, riboflavin, iron, copper, calcium and folic acid. Beets stimulate the appetite, relieve headaches and are easily digestible. Beets combat colds and anemia. Beet juice clears up acne.

Cabbage

Cabbage is best in the fall. Savoy cabbage is yellow-green and excellent in soups or as a side dish. Red cabbage has a dark purple tint and complements salads well. White cabbage has tight leaves and is good for cole slaw and sauerkraut. White cabbage is not as tasty or delicate as Savoy or Red cabbage.

When buying a cabbage, choose one that is compact and heavy for its size. A cabbage should have shiny, well-colored leaves that are free of cracks and bruises. Store cabbage in a perforated plastic bag and it will keep for 2 weeks. As cabbage ages, its odor becomes more pronounced.

When boiling red cabbage, a little vinegar in the water will prevent the cabbage from losing its color. Over-cooked cabbage tends to lose its color, nutrients and acquires an unpleasant taste.

Cabbage is an excellent source of vitamin C and folic acid. It is also a good source of potassium and vitamin B. Cabbage is an excellent cleanser of the teeth and the digestive system. An anti-diarreal, antibiotic, and remineralizer, cabbage also stimulates the appetite. Cabbage combats scurvy and contains numerous anti-cancer, antioxidant compounds. The leaves of cabbage contain the most nutrients in their raw form.

Capers

These wonderful pods are full of flavor. The smaller capers are more aromatic. Once opened, a jar of capers requires refrigeration.

Capers improve digestion and stimulate the appetite. They also act as a tonic and a diuretic.

Cardamom

Native to India, cardamom is the pod of a perennial plant of the ginger family. Although cardamom is one of the most expensive spices, it is essential in many spice blends. Cardamom is found in Massaman paste, Ras al Hanout and Garam Masala.

Cardamom is best bought whole and ground as needed. Used in savory as well as sweet dishes, cardamom aids digestion. Cardamom stimulates the appetite. Chewing cardamom seeds freshens the breath.

Carrots

This extremely versatile vegetable reaches its peak in the springtime. Carrots give stocks and soups both flavor and color. Carrots are one of the most nutritious vegetables.

Buy carrots that are firm and brightly colored. Deep orange carrots have the most disease fighting antioxidants. If the root is green, the carrot has been exposed to sunlight. When storing carrots, remove their roots as they absorb moisture. Refrigerate carrots in a towel in a perforated plastic bag. The cooler the storing temperature, the longer carrots will preserve their flavor.

Carrots are an excellent source of vitamin A and potassium. They also contain vitamin B6, copper, folic acid and magnesium. Carrots lower one's chances of heart attacks, as well as fight angina. Carrots treat constipation and depress blood cholesterol. The nutrients in carrots fight a variety of cancers, including stomach, lung, endometrial and larynx. Carrots protect the arteries, boost the immune system, fight infections, and substantially reduce the chances of cataracts. Thoroughly chew carrots to receive the maximum nutrients.

Celery

This summer vegetable adds a delightful texture and flavor to a variety of dishes. Golden celery or celery heart is the best type to eat raw. Green celery is strongly flavored and best for cooking.

When shopping for celery, choose stalks with healthy green leaves. Flexibility in celery indicates staleness. Refrigerate celery wrapped in a towel and it will keep for a week. Celery also keeps well standing in cold, salted water.

Celery is easier to digest if peeled before consumption. Celery is a mild diuretic. It is the Vietnamese remedy for high blood pressure. Celery contains 8 families of anticancer compounds that detoxify carcinogens. This vegetable cleanses the system, prevents scurvy, remineralizes the body and reduces hormones associated with stress. Celery stimulates the appetite. Celery is also a stomachic, antiseptic, antirheumatic, tonic and a hangover cure.

Chickpeas

Also known as the garbanzo bean, the chickpea is the fruit of an annual herbaceous plant believed to have originated in the Middle East. Its Latin name *arietinum*, means small ram and alludes to the shape of the bean being the shape of a ram's head. Soak chickpeas for 12 hours before cooking them. Simmer the beans for 2 - 2.5 hours. In the Middle East, chickpeas are used for hummus and falafel. In the South of France, chefs make estouffade, cocido and puchero with chickpeas.

Chickpeas are an excellent source of folic acid and potassium. They also act as a diuretic and an intestinal cleanser. The high vitamin B-1 content in chickpeas causes an increase in appetite in undernourished persons.

Endive

The endive season lasts from October to March. The slightly bitter taste of endive gives complexity to salads. Yellow endive can be braised, steamed or roasted. Red endive should not be cooked, as it loses its color and flavor.

Choose endives with compact heads and creamy leaves. The ideal endive is five times as long as it is wide. Avoid any endive that appears wilted or browning.

Store endive in a perforated bag or wrapped in a damp cloth. If properly stored, endive will keep for up to seven days.

Before using, rinse endive leaves under cold running water. Do not soak endive, as this tends to augment its bitterness. Remove the core from the endive and the leaves should fall away easily.

Endive is an excellent source of folic acid. It also contains potassium, vitamin C, pantothenic acid, riboflavin and zinc. Endive cleanses the system, aids the liver, acts as a tonic and remineralizes the body. These delicious leaves aid in digestion as well as stimulate the appetite.

Fennel

The peppery taste of fennel complements fish and poultry. This Italian bulb ripens in the winter.

When buying fennel, avoid yellow, tired-looking bulbs. Choose firm, fragrant, white, unblemished specimens with bright green stalks. Fennel will keep for a week in the refrigerator but it tends to become stringy with age.

Remove the rough outer leaves and the core from a fennel bulb before preparing it. Fennel bulbs can be eaten raw or cooked. The stalks flavor stocks and sauces but are too potent for raw consumption.

An excellent source of potassium, fennel also provides vitamin C, folic acid, magnesium, calcium and phosphorus. Fennel acts as a diuretic, an antispasmodic and a stimulant. Fennel stimulates the appetite, soothes gastric pain, aids in the digestion of fatty foods, cleanses the system and prevents flatulence.

Lentils

This flavorful legume is the seed of the annual herbaceous plant. This plant originated in central Asia. Lentils have been enjoyed since prehistoric times and was one of the first foods grown by man.

Unlike most legumes, lentils do not require a soaking time. Wash them carefully and remove any stones. While brown lentils take about 60 minutes to cook, orange lentils take only 20-30 minutes. Lentils are a welcome addition to soups and lentil purée is often used to make croquettes.

Lentils are an excellent source of folic acid and potassium. Lentils also stimulate the appetite in those who have not consumed enough nutrients to generate hunger.

Lettuce

Lettuce is at its best in the springtime. Butter, Bibb or Boston lettuce has delicate leaves and flavor. Leaf lettuce is tender and flavorful. Imperative to Caesar salads, Romaine lettuce has a crisp and fibrous central rib. Celtuce is an Asian delicacy that is a cross between celery and lettuce. Head or iceberg lettuce is less colorful and nutritious than other varieties.

When buying lettuce, choose a head with firm glossy leaves. Avoid yellow or brown leaves. The greener the lettuce, the more nutritious it is.

Lettuce is rich in folic acid. Lettuce stimulates the appetite. Lettuce is an emollient and a sedative. Recommended for insomnia and nervous or sexual excitement, lettuce also acts as a cough remedy.

Mango

This refreshing fruit reaches its peak in the summer. Common in the United States are the orange-fleshed Hayden mango and the yellow-fleshed Tommy Atkins mango. The Pakistani Alphonse or Indian mango tastes like a nectarine.

When buying a mango, choose an unbruised fruit with a soft yet firm flesh, smooth skin and a fruit aroma around the stem. Avoid mangoes that are very soft, bruised, have black spots, are very green or rock hard. Prematurely picked mangoes are shriveled, have a fibrous meat and an acidic skin.

Mangoes will ripen at room temperature, but this process is hastened by placing the mango in a paper bag. Ripe mangoes will keep refrigerated for 1-2 weeks.

The seed of a mango is slightly oval and flat. Remove the flesh from a mango by cutting around this seed.

An excellent source of vitamin A, mangoes also supply copper and potassium. When unripe mangoes have a laxative effect. The high zinc content of mangoes help stimulate the appetite.

Melon

A treat at any time, melon is delicious alone or complementing a wide variety of dishes. Before serving melon, let it stand at room temperature and it will become more aromatic.

There are many types of melon including the orange-fleshed Cantaloupes, Prince melons and Muskmelons. The flesh of the Honeydew melon changes from green to creamy yellow as it ripens. The less fragrant Casaba melon has wrinkled yellow or orange skin with a whitish flesh. Persian melons have darkish green skins and form brown nettings at maturity. Canary melons have yellow skin and a whitish flesh, that turns pink near the cavity.

The Ogen melons have smooth, ribbed skin with greenish-yellow coloring. The flesh of the Ogen is either deep pink or pale green. With brownish, ribbed and netted skin, the Galia melon has a very aromatic pale green flesh. The festive Santa Claus melon is yellow with black and green stripes.

When buying a melon, inspect it carefully for signs of ripeness. Regardless of variety, a melon is not mature if the stalk end is very hard, unevenly colored or part of the greenish stalk is still attached. The end opposite of the stalk should have a delicate aroma. Ripe melons will make a hollow sound when tapped.

If a portion of melon is unused, leave the seeds in it to prevent it from drying out. Melons should be left at room temperature to ripen. Melons release an abundance of ethylene gas which can ripen other fruits.

Melon is an excellent source of potassium. It also contains vitamin C and folic acid. Melon is reinvigorating. This delicious fruit is a diuretic and a laxative. Melon stimulates the appetite and has anticoagulant activity.

Oregano

This herb gives more flavor in its dried form than when it is fresh. When buying fresh oregano, look for firm stems.

Oregano supplies the body with calcium, potassium, magnesium and iron. Oregano is an antispasmodic, antiseptic, bactericidal, stomachic, expectorant and a sedative. Oregano alleviates colic, facilitates digestion and is beneficial on the respiratory system. Oregano stimulates the appetite and eases migraines, car sickness and bronchitis.

Parsley

Parsley may be the most widely used herb today. Curly parsley has bright green leaves and long stems. Flat leaf or Italian parsley has flat, dark leaves that have a highly fragrant taste. Flat leaf parsley tends to be less bitter than curly parsley.

Avoid parsley that is yellow, brown or wilted. Keep parsley refrigerated in a perforated plastic bag with a damp paper towel. Swish parsley leaves in cold water to remove any dirt.

Add parsley at the last minute to preserve its color, flavor and nutrients. Parsley stems add a pleasant flavor to stocks, soups and sauces.

Parsley contains potassium, calcium, phosphorus and vitamins C and A. This versatile herb acts as a diuretic and a stimulant. Parsley stimulates the appetite, aids digestion and combats scurvy and intestinal problems. Eating a sprig of parsley eliminates garlic breath.

Radicchio

Winter is the season for these bitter leaves. The magenta leaves of Radicchio beautify any plate. Originally, Radicchio leaves are green but they turn red when the temperature drops.

Radicchio di Verona has a round head and short red leaves, with white stalks and veins. This strain has a slightly bitter taste that complements salads. Imported from Italy, Radicchio di Treviso has long, thin red leaves and a long thick root. Cooking intensifies the peppery taste of this strain.

When buying raddichio, choose firm, compact heads that lack brown edges. Radicchio will keep for one week refrigerated in a perforated plastic bag.

Radicchio contains folic acid, potassium, copper and vitamin C. This miniature cabbage stimulates the appetite, cleanses the blood and remineralizes the body. Radicchio also acts as a diuretic, a stomachic and a tonic.

Radish

This winter vegetable comes in a variety of colors, shapes and degrees of bite. The Red Globe is red, round and crisp with a juicy white flesh. The rough greens are edible and should be prepared as spinach. The long black radish is very sharp and should be used sparingly. Daikon is mild and best used raw. Daikon is usually white but can be pink, green or black.

When buying radishes choose firm, smooth skinned ones with no cracks or blemishes. Look for bright green leaves. Avoid larger specimens as they tend to be more fibrous and have a sharper flavor.

Radishes will keep for a week, if refrigerated in a perforated plastic bag. Remove the greens from the radishes, as they tend to accelerate the loss of moisture.

Radishes tend to lose their pungency once cut; thus cut radishes just prior to serving them. A splash of vinegar or lemon juice in the cooking liquid will enhance the color of red radishes. Conversely, baking soda discolors red radishes. Lime juice, salt and freshly ground pepper accentuate the sweetness of a radish.

Radishes are good sources of vitamin C and potassium. Radishes act as antiseptics, antiarthritics and antirheumatics. Radishes combat scurvy and rickets. These refreshing vegetables stimulate the appetite and aid in digestion. Radishes are used in the treatment of asthma, bronchitis, mineral deficiencies and liver and gall bladder troubles.

Rye

Rye is a cereal grain that is native to Asia Minor. There are about a dozen species and many varieties of rye. Having a gluten that is less elastic and that retains less gas causes rye bread to be denser than wheat bread. Rye bread also keeps longer than wheat bread.

Store rye flour in an air-tight container in a dry cool place. Whether light or dark, rye flour is an excellent source of magnesium and thiamine. Rye flour helps control high blood pressure, arteriosclerosis and vascular disease.

Sage

This herb has a distinctive flavor that is imperative in breakfast sausage. To preserve its flavor, add fresh sage at the end of the cooking process.

Sage is a tonic, an antispasmodic, an antiseptic and a diuretic. Sage stimulates the appetite, has cleansing properties and is effective against mouth sores and sore throats. Sage also stimulates menstruation and relieves flatulence.

Sesame Seeds

Sesame seeds are thought to be the first condiment and the first plant used for its edible oil. The phrase "open sesame" evolved from the sesame seeds' tendency to burst out of their hulls when they are mature.

Half of the weight of sesame seeds is their oil. Sesame oil has a very high smoking point and is extremely resistant to rancidity.

Sesame seeds are sold raw or roasted and with or without hulls. Refrigerate hulled seeds and store whole seeds in an air-tight container away from heat and humidity.

Sesame seeds are an excellent source of magnesium, potassium, iron, calcium, phosphorus, zinc, copper, thiamine, niacin, folic acid and vitamin B 6. These seeds increase the appetite in malnourished persons. Sesame seeds act as a laxative, an antiarthritic and an emollient. Beneficial to the nervous system, sesame seeds also aid digestion and activate blood circulation.

Shallots

An integral ingredient in French cuisine, the shallot is a tasty member of the lily family. The gray shallot is small and slender with gray skin and a purple head. The Cuisse de Poulet shallot has an elongated bulb with copper colored skin. The Jersey shallot has a short round bulb, pink skin and veiny flesh. The Jersey shallot has a milder taste than its brothers.

Shallots are less harsh than garlic and more subtle than onions. Shallots are less potent than onions because of their thinner layers. In the spring, shallots grow green ends that can be used in place of chives.

When shopping for shallots, buy those with firm and dry skins. Avoid any soft, sprouted or blemished shallots. Shallots will keep for a month in a dry, dark, cool, well-ventilated area. If kept in the refrigerator, these bulbs will only last 2 weeks.

When cutting shallots, do not remove the skin and root on one's cutting board. The exterior of a shallot harbors an abundance of dirt, which can easily stick to one's cutting surface. This dirt can get into one's dish and result in a sandy texture.

Cooking shallots with a pinch of salt, helps them release their juices. Shallots give an extraordinary flavor to sauces. Unfortunately, browned shallots make a sauce unpleasantly bitter.

Shallots are rich in minerals. Shallots stimulate the appetite. This delicious bulb acts as a stimulant. A raw shallot cut in half can relieve burns and insect bites.

Tarragon

This peppery herb lends a kick to any bland dish. The Russian strain is much more pungent than French tarragon.

Regardless of strain, use tarragon with caution as it tends to overwhelm a dish. If using whole leaves, you could blanch them in boiling, salted water first. This will take the edge off of the taste.

Tarragon supplies the body with potassium, calcium, magnesium, phosphorus and iron. Tarragon acts as a diuretic, antiseptic, carminative, vermifuge and an antispasmodic. Tarragon regulates menstruation and stimulates digestion and the appetite.

Tomatoes

This summer fruit tastes wonderful alone and complements any dish. The best tomatoes appear at the end of summer. If using tomatoes at the end of the summer, omit the tomato paste a recipe may suggest.

In the market, choose tomatoes that are firm, smooth, pleasant smelling and free of bruises. Refrigerate tomatoes only to chill them. Refrigeration tends to diminish tomatoes' flavor and soften their texture. Tomatoes are best left on a window sill to ripen.

Tomatoes are low in sodium and rich in vitamins A and C. Tomatoes also supply potassium and folic acid. This fruit acts as a diuretic and a mineralizer. Tomatoes stimulate the appetite, combat scurvy and cleanse the system of toxins. Tomatoes are a major source of lycopene, which is a substantial antioxidant and anticancer agent.

Watercress

As with most greens, watercress reaches its peak in summer. These round leaves yield a slightly pungent, peppery flavor complementing any salad.

When buying watercress look for leaves of a deep green color. Choose bunches with small tender stems and avoid wilted, yellow or spotted leaves.

Do not wash watercress until just prior to use. Swirl the leaves in a bowl of cold water until they are free of dirt.

Watercress is an excellent source of potassium, vitamin A and vitamin C. Watercress also contains calcium, magnesium, riboflavin, vitamin B6 and phosphorus. This tender green acts as a diuretic, remineralizer and an antianemic. Watercress stimulates the appetite, cleanses the intestines and combats scurvy. Chewing watercress releases a substance that neutralizes a carcinogen in cigarette smoke.

Recipes

Anchovy Wrapped Capers with Mozzarella
    and Olive Tapenade on Zucchini Slices 34
Asparagus, Basil, Mozzarella and Serrano Ham Rolls 143

Barbecue Pork with Pineapple Sage Salsa on Goat Cheese Biscuits 136
Basil and Pink Grapefruit Scallops with Mixed Greens on Anise Crackers 85
Beef Tenderloin with Fresh Herb Pesto on Oregano Biscuits 122
Beef Tenderloin with Tomato and Caper Relish on Chili Bagels 124
Beef Tenderloin, Corn Salsa and Jack Cheese Quesadillas 120
Beef, Pecan and Radicchio Strudel 119
Black Bean Cakes with Beet Cream 22
Boiled Crawfish with Cantaloupe Papaya Salad on Sesame Crackers 78
Braised Beef and Carrots with Bibb Lettuce in French Rolls 126
Buffalo Patties with Radicchio Sauce on Cilantro Pita Chips 165

Cajun Smoked Duck Breast with Fennel on Tangy Chive Toasts 167
Cantaloupe and Papaya Salad with Prosciutto in Plums 144
Cantaloupe and Papaya Slices with Goat Cheese on Carrot Nut Bread 28
Caramelized Apricot Slices with Camembert on Pumpernickel Toasts 23
Cardamom Scallops with Celeriac Purée on Brown Bread 86
Catfish and Basil Sausage with Cantaloupe Sauce on Sesame Pita Chips 40
Catfish Nuggets with Raspberry Dipping Sauce 39
Celeriac Purée with Shiitake Mushrooms
    and Rendered Bacon in Phyllo Dough 138
Chicken and Grapefruit Salad in Oat Rolls 104
Chicken Breast and Carrot Rolls 100
Chicken Egg Rolls with Apricot Sauce 98
Clam and Corn Fritters with Blue Cheese and Basil Dressing 74
Coconut Pork with Basil and Mango on Pita Chips .140
Confit of Duck with Spinach and Basil in Phyllo Dough 171
Crab Salad in Lettuce Pouches 84
Crab Tempura with Spicy Tomato Dipping Sauce 81
Crabmeat, Capers and Fennel Stuffed in Mushroom Caps 83
Cured Salmon with Fennel Cream on Cucumber Slices 42

Duck Sausage Rolls with Sweet Mustard Sauce 169

Fish Cakes with Tropical Dipping Sauce 62
Fresh Herb Clam Stuffing on Bagel Chips with Roasted Red Peppers 72
Fresh Herb Pâté with Oregano Mustard on Gouda-Thyme Bread 145
Fried Quail Legs with Spicy Lemon Grass Sauce 152

Ginger Chicken with Radicchio and Lentil Salad on Sweet Toasts 102
Glazed Radishes with Black Bean Purée 29
Glazed Shrimp with Oregano Roasted Shallots on French Bread 75
Green Crawfish Cakes with Roasted Red Pepper Aioli 80
Green Peppercorn Crusted Tuna with Wasabi Aioli on Carrot Crackers 56

Julienne of Chicken Breast with Braised Caper
    and Tomato Sauce on Fresh Herb Focaccia 96

Leek and Carrot Rolls Stuffed with Fennel and Comté
    Dressed with Champagne Vinaigrette 25

Mahi Mahi with Mango Salsa and Caper Aioli on Crusty Buttermilk Toasts 58
Marinated Asparagus with Smoked Gouda and Eggplant 20
Marinated Goat Cheese with Lentil Salad on Anadama Toasts 14
Miniature Cabbage and Roasted Shallot Quiches 12
Mint Pesto Stuffed Lamb with Shaved Fennel 130
Miso Lobster with Endive Chiffonade in Choux Pastry 91

Oregano Sausage with Tomatoes and Olive Tapenade on Cheese Biscuits 147
Oyster, Bacon and Carrot Brochettes with Caper Tartar 68
Oysters Baked on the Half Shell with Tarragon and Bacon Cream Sauce 66
Oysters Served on the Half Shell with Roasted Beet Vinaigrette 67

Pickled Clams with Tomato and Oregano Relish on Wonton Chips 70
Pita Wraps of Sesame Mahi Mahi with Watercress .60
Poached Halibut with Tarragon Sauce and Lettuce Leaves on Walnut Toasts 47
Poppy Seed Dusted Sea Bass with Radish Slaw on Wonton Chips 64
Pork Tenderloin Stuffed with Sage, Salami,
    Asparagus and Roasted Red Peppers 142
Potato Crusted Halibut with Fennel Relish on Sour Cream Toasts 49
Prosciutto and Goat Cheese Wrapped Cantaloupe Slices 139
Prosciutto Stuffed Halibut with Radicchio on Cornmeal Toasts 51

Quail Tamales with Tomato and Avocado Salsa 150

Rabbit Sausage with Garlic Roasted Shallots on Oregano Focaccia 162
Rabbit, Tarragon and Sunflower Seed Terrine
      with Glazed Parsnips on Dill Toasts 160
Red Cabbage Chiffonade with Apple Chutney and Walnuts on Herb Toasts 31
Roasted Jalapeños with Corn and Cheddar Stuffing 17
Roasted Quail with Avocado and Tomato Cream on Tomatillo Tortilla Chips . .154
Rock Shrimp Wontons with Spicy Honey 77

Scallop Seviche with Tomato and Avocado Salsa on Whole Wheat Toasts 89
Sesame and Black Pepper Crusted Beef
      with Carrot and Endive Slaw on Pita Chips 128
Skirt Steak with Mango Salsa 118
Sliced Loin of Lamb with Oregano Hummus on Pumpkin Crackers 132
Sliced Rabbit with Carrot Relish on Rye Toasts 158
Smoked Chicken Salad in Endive Leaves 108
Smoked Pheasant with Hummus on Parmesan Biscuits 156
Smoked Salmon Cakes with Jalapeño Tartar 43
Smoked Trout and Tomato Quiches 35
Smoked Turkey Breast with Sweet Beet Slices
      on Half-Cracked Black Pepper Crackers 114
Spicy Glazed Scallops 88
Spicy Tuna with Carrot and Cucumber Slaw on Chapati Crisps 53
Spicy Turkey Breast with Cantaloupe on Parmesan Toasts 109
Spinach Rolls with Basil, Mozzarella and Tomato Confit 26
Spinach, Carrot and Beet Terrine of Sole with Cumin Sesame Crackers 44
Split Green Pea Patties with Tomato Yogurt Dipping Sauce 18
Steamed Mussels with Cucumber Cardamom Sauce 93

Tarragon Chicken Wings with Caper Mayonnaise 106
Trout with Avocado Purée on Sesame Crackers 37
Tuna Nori Rolls with Carrot, Radish, Avocado and Tobiko 55
Turkey Kibbe Kebabs with Mint Basil Dressing 116
Turkey Patties with Tomato Confit and Scallion Aioli on Basil Bagels 111

White Bean, Red Onion and Basil Stuffed Cherry Tomatoes 16